How Anyone Can STOP PAYING Income Taxes

Irwin Schiff's

How Anyone Can STOP PAYING Income Taxes

with

Howy Murzin

Freedom Books

Hamden, Connecticut

Library of Congress Catalog Card No. 81-71431
ISBN-0-930374-03-7

82 83 84 85 10 9 8 7 6 5 4 3 2 1

To
the misled and intimidated
American Taxpayer
who is about to be emancipated.

Contents

INTRODUCTION 11

1. Surprise! The Income Tax is Voluntary! 13

2. The Federal Government is Required to
   Determine Your Income Tax 23

3. The Internal Revenue Code—A Masterpiece of Deception 31

4. How the IRS Violates the Law 41

5. How to Stop Paying Income Taxes 61

6. No One Need Submit to an IRS Audit 77

7. How the Public Gets Brainwashed 95

8. Federal Judges—The Real Culprits 115

9. Why *Not* Filing is in the Nation's
   Interest 133

   Epilogue 143
   Appendix 172

INTRODUCTION

In 1980, ninety-three million Americans were tricked into filing and paying federal income taxes, when legally they didn't have to do either. If this statement shocks you, it is only because you and the rest of the nation's taxpayers have been thoroughly deceived by the federal government and an army of accountants, lawyers, and other tax preparers—all of whom have a substantial financial interest in keeping you ignorant concerning the real nature of federal income taxes.

That millions of supposedly intelligent Americans could be thoroughly convinced that they are legally required to file and pay income taxes each year, when such is not the case, must rank as the greatest and most spectacular hoax of all time. In many ways, the spectacle of millions of Americans scurrying to IRS offices each April fifteenth resembles the lemmings' march to the sea.

But, as Abe Lincoln is reputed to have said, "You can fool all of the people some of the time, and some of the people all of the time, but you can't fool all of the people all of the time." And now, this deception will be brought to an end. Before you finish reading this book you will know that—

1. no American is legally required to file an income tax return;
2. no American is legally required to submit to a tax audit; and
3. no American is legally required to have income taxes taken out of his pay or to pay quarterly tax estimates.

I know that all of this is hard to believe and is contrary to everything you ever thought you knew about federal income taxes, but the proof is all here. So read on, you're not dreaming.

1

Surprise! The Income Tax is Voluntary

> The United States has a system of taxation by confession.
>
> Supreme Court Justice Hugo Black

Would you believe that there is no section of the Internal Revenue Code that requires you to file a tax return? Well, it's true; so if you file tax returns, you do so "voluntarily."

Indeed, every offical government statement on this subject admits to the voluntary nature of the income tax system, as the following statements of former IRS commissioners indicate:

> The IRS's primary task is to collect taxes under a *voluntary compliance* system. (emphasis added)
>
>> Jerome Kurtz
>> Internal Revenue Annual Report, 1980

> Our tax system is based on individual *self-assessment* and *voluntary compliance*. (emphasis added)
>
>> Mortimer Caplin
>> Internal Revenue Audit Manual, 1975

> Each year American taxpayers *voluntarily file* their tax returns and make a special effort to pay the taxes they owe. (emphasis added)
>
>> Johnnie M. Walters
>> Internal Revenue 1040 Booklet, 1971

Even the United States Supreme Court has held that the income tax system is voluntary:

> Our tax system is based upon *voluntary assessment and payment,* not upon distraint[1] (emphasis added)
>
>> *Flora v. United States*[2] (1959)

Since, as you will discover, compliance with federal income taxes is voluntary, the objective of the federal government is to confuse and intimidate the public on this issue so as to convince it that compliance is not voluntary but compulsory. The ability of a government to convince a vast population that it *must* behave in a manner that is opposite to the requirements of its own laws is not something out of a George Orwell novel but a reality of contemporary American life.

The Meaning of "Voluntary Compliance"

No matter how many dictionaries you check, you'll discover that the word "voluntary" means *something done of one's own free will and without legal obligation.* Some representative definitions are:

> acting or done without any present legal obligation to do the thing done
>> Webster's Third World International Dictionary

---

1. "Distraint" means to take property by force (see page 64).
2. Complete citings on page 179.

acting or performing without legal obligation
> American Heritage Dictionary

performed without legal obligation
> Funk and Wagnalls Standard College Dictionary

So if you file and pay income taxes, you do so as a matter of free choice and without any legal obligation to do so. Is that what you thought when you labored over *your* tax returns? Chances are, if you are like most Americans, you thought that filing and paying income taxes was compulsory.

The Fifth Amendment or, Why Filing An Income Tax Return Can Not Be Compulsory

There are probably more misconceptions about the Fifth Amendment than about any other provision in the United States Constitution—for the simple reason that the public is perhaps more familiar with this amendment than any other section of the Constitution because of the attention it has received on television.

Much of the problem is due to the fact that those who claim the Fifth Amendment on television generally do so by saying, "I plead the Fifth Amendment and refuse to answer the question on the grounds that the answer might tend to incriminate me," or words to that effect. Thus, the public has come to believe that the Fifth Amendment only protects individuals against self-incrimination and nothing more. However, "self-incrimination" has absolutely nothing to do with your Fifth Amendment right. As a matter of fact, self-incrimination is not even mentioned in the amendment, which declares that "no person shall . . . be compelled in any criminal case to be a witness against himself."

So the amendment states that you cannot be compelled to be a witness and give information about yourself, *whether or not such information is incriminating*. This means that under no circumstances can the government require you to provide it with information which it can use against you for an alleged violation of a civil or criminal statute. Although the Fifth Amendment mentions only "criminal matters," the Supreme Court has ruled that the Fifth Amendment "applies alike to criminal and civil proceedings."[3]

Self-incrimination has nothing to do with your Fifth Amendment right not to be compelled to be a witness against yourself because you might not know *which* information you divulge could be incriminating. The founding fathers' abhorrence for compelling individuals to give information about themselves goes right back to their abhorrence of the medieval rack, which authorities used to torture individuals in order to extract confessions. Any process, therefore, by which the government forces citizens to give information about themselves, which can later be used to punish them in any way, is an extension of the "rack" mentality and is thus barred by the United States Constitution.

Self-Incrimination has Nothing to do with Your Tax Return

The public's confusion concerning its Fifth Amendment right and the far-better-known Fifth Amendment privilege against self-incrimination, is due

3. *McCarthy* v. *Arndstein*

to the American legal principle that "the state is entitled to everyone's testimony."

This is a good principle, since it is designed to protect the innocent and convict the guilty. Suppose, for example, that you were charged with a crime, but the testimony of another person could establish your innocence. Shouldn't you have the right to compel that person to testify at your trial to help prove your innocence? The answer is yes—which is why both parties in a criminal trial have the power to subpoena witnesses. Without being subpoenaed, many witnesses might refuse to testify, but a subpoenaed witness must testify or risk being held in contempt of court. Similarly, congressional committees have the power to subpoena witnesses in connection with congressional investigations. What should be noted in all of these examples is that those subpoenaed are not the subjects, or "targets," of the inquiries. Their testimonies are only needed because they reflect on *other* people and on matters not directly related to themselves.

However, if, in this situation, questions are asked to which the answers might be incriminating, the witness can refuse to answer. In such instances the witness claims, not his Fifth Amendment *right* not to be compelled to witness against himself, but his Fifth Amendment *privilege* against self-incrimination, since, in that setting, he has no right *not* to be a witness. Note that in one case we have the claim of a *right* which can have no exceptions, while in the other case we have the claim of a *privilege* which can have exceptions, such as the granting of immunity to a witness in exchange for his testimony.

What has all this to do with your tax return? It is precisely the Fifth Amendment that bars the federal government from requiring you to file a tax return, since

any information on a tax return can be used against you.
This fact was clearly recognized by a United States
Court of Appeals in 1926 in the case of *Sullivan* v. *United
States*, as follows:

> There can be no question that one who files a return under oath
> is a witness within the meaning of the Amendment.

In 1976, the United States Supreme Court reiterated
this when it held in *Garner* v. *United States:*

> The information revealed in the preparation and filing of an
> income tax return is, for Fifth Amendment analysis, the tes-
> timony of a "witness" as that term is used herein.

So United States courts have consistently held that
those who submit tax returns are witnesses against themselves within the meaning of the Fifth Amendment—
and the United States government *cannot require that
anyone be a witness against himself within the meaning
of the Fifth Amendment.*

It should not come as a surprise that those who file
tax returns are witnesses against themselves, since returns are signed under penalty of perjury and are routinely used against taxpayers, especially those prosecuted for income tax evasion. In such prosecutions, the
taxpayer's return is introduced at his trial and is the very
instrument used to gain the taxpayer's conviction.

What the public has overlooked is that filing a tax
return under penalty of perjury is tantamount to taking
the witness stand at your own trial and giving testimony
that can be used against you. It is precisely this sworn
testimony that the government uses against taxpayers
when it prosecutes them for "tax crimes" and even
crimes which are unrelated to taxes.

Since the Constitution states that Americans cannot be required to provide such information against themselves, there can be no provision in the Internal Revenue Code requiring anyone to file a tax return. Of course, you can file one if you want to. But did anybody advise you that when you filed your tax return, you did so voluntarily and that, in so doing, you were actually waiving a constitutional right?

Tax Returns Can be Used Against You

A good example of how tax returns can be used against you is the aforementioned Garner case, in which Garner indicated on his tax return that he was a professional gambler. Sometime later, Garner was prosecuted along with several others for violating federal gambling laws. When he attempted at his trial to maintain that he was not a gambler, the government introduced his tax return (on which he had admitted to being a gambler) and used it to convict him. Garner subsequently appealed to the Supreme Court on the grounds that the information on his tax return should not have been used against him. He claimed that the information on his return was required, that it was *compelled*, and so using the information against him was a violation of the Fifth Amendment.

The Supreme Court thought otherwise. They held that the information on a tax return is supplied *voluntarily* and affirmed Garner's conviction, stating that he had supplied the information as a matter of "free choice." In short, because he gave the information voluntarily, it could be used against him.

If we compare Garner's dilemma to a normal police interrogation, it becomes obvious that giving information to the IRS is like giving information to a policeman after he has arrested you and read you your rights. For example, let us assume that before being interrogated, an officer tells you that you have a right to remain silent and warns you that anything you say can be used against you. The officer advises you that you don't have to give him any information, but if you do, the information can be used against you at a trial.

Had the police officer in this example not read you your "Miranda Rights," or had he extracted the information from you by force, the information could not be used against you since compelled testimony cannot be used against an individual in a trial. Similarly, if information on a tax return were forced from people, i.e., if people could be fined or sent to jail if they didn't give it, the government could not use such information in tax prosecutions—or in any other prosecution, for that matter. It is *only* because the information on a tax return is considered to have been given *voluntarily* that the government can use it against individuals in criminal and civil cases. This, then, is proof that the information you give on your tax return is voluntary.

Since the information on a tax return is given freely, and since it can be used against those who file, taxpayers must be given a warning similar to that given by the police officer in our "Miranda Rights" example. Although most taxpayers are unaware of that warning, it can be found in your 1040 Booklet tucked away in the Privacy Act Notice.

The Taxpayer's Miranda Warning— The Privacy Act Notice

The Privacy Act Notice (Page 42) found in a 1040 Booklet is comparable to the Miranda warning given by a police officer. Note that it warns the taxpayer (at Note

D) that all information on his* return can be turned over to the Department of Justice or numerous other agencies, all of whom are free, of course, to use the information against him. This is the taxpayer's notice that he does not have to supply the information, since Americans are supposed to know that their government cannot require them to give information which can be used against them in this manner. Specifically, it is Section 6103 (*h* and *i*) of the Internal Revenue Code that provides that all information on tax returns can be turned over to the Department of Justice and used against the taxpayer in all manner of criminal and civil proceedings.

Getting back to the Garner case, his problem was that he, like millions of other Americans, did not realize that when he filed a tax return he voluntarily waived his Fifth Amendment right and "volunteered" to become a witness against himself by giving the government information that it could use against him. Thus Garner, like numerous other Americans, went to jail because he made the mistake of sending in a tax return.

Can The Government Ever Require You To Be A Witness Against Yourself?

The answer to the above caption is a very definite *NO*. Congress cannot pass a law (tax or otherwise) that can infringe upon your Fifth Amendment right. The Supreme Court ruled in the landmark Miranda decision that—

> The Fifth Amendment provision that the individual cannot be compelled to be a witness against himself cannot be abridged.

*The terms he and him as used in this book are meant to include both genders.

and that—

> Where rights secured by the Constitution are involved, there
> can be no rule-making or legislation which would abrogate
> them.

So, (1) the Fifth Amendment states that the federal
government cannot require anyone to be a witness
against himself; (2) the Supreme Court has ruled that
those who file tax returns are witnesses against themselves; and (3) Congress can make no law abridging a
constitutional right. In view of this, Congress can clearly
make no law requiring anyone to file a tax return. This is
why the filing of an income tax return is an act that we
Americans do only on a voluntary basis. This principle is
so clear that it cannot be challenged on any basis.

If, therefore, you filed a tax return, believing that it
was *required*, you had a false impression. Just how you
acquired this impression will be the subject of other parts
of this book, but at least you now know that, come next
April fifteenth, you don't *have to* file a tax return. If you
want to, okay—but legally you are not, and cannot be,
required to do so!

2

The Federal Government is Required to Determine Your Income Tax

To lay with one hand the power of the government on the property of the citizen, and with the other to bestow it on favored individuals ...is none the less *robbery* because it is done under the forms of law and is called taxation.

United States Supreme Court
Loan Association v. *Topeka* (1874)

Since private citizens are not required to file tax returns, it must, therefore, be the federal government's responsibility to figure out your taxes, and that is precisely what the law provides! Despite this, ninety-three million Americans actually believe that it is their responsibility to figure out their own taxes; so they expend needless time and money doing it. It is estimated that over thirty million Americans even seek trained professional help in order to calculate their own taxes for the benefit of the federal government.

Citizens would be appalled if, instead of sending out property tax notices, city and town governments sent out instructional manuals asking private citizens to compute their own taxes, under the penalty of perjury. Such manuals might describe how property values had to be adjusted to reflect various alternate methods of depreciation. They might also describe how to determine the proper method of depreciation, and how alterations and improvements (inside and out) might affect this value—given the absence of appropriate market values. Suppose that such manuals referred to formulas for adjusting property values (taking into consideration such things as original cost, replacement cost, and potential market value). Formulas might be affected by many things—heating, plumbing, electrical systems—so, in order not to break the law, property owners would need to seek out, at their own expense, professional assessors to help them determine their property taxes. Then, after the privately hired assessor determined the correct property taxes, using formulas and calculations unfamiliar to the taxpayer, the taxpayer would be required to sign this complicated property tax return "under penalty of perjury," thereby certifying that his tax liability was "true and correct," and that it conformed to a set of laws that he didn't understand. Could local governments get away with levying property taxes like that? Of course not. This, however, is exactly the manner in which the federal government goes about "levying" income taxes.

While the Sixteenth Amendment is regarded as providing the basis for an "income" tax, it nevertheless clearly states that such taxes can be collected only after they have first been assessed.[1] The federal government must clearly "lay" an income tax on a citizen before he can be expected to pay it. Merely sending a citizen a

1. The Sixteenth Amendment reads as follows: "The Congress shall have the power to *lay* and collect taxes on incomes . . ." (emphasis added)

schedule of applicable tax rates with instructions on how to compute one's own taxes does not constitute the "laying" or "assessing" of a tax—and citizens are under no legal obligation to lay or assess taxes on themselves! As we previously established, the Internal Revenue Code contains no provisions requiring citizens to submit tax returns, so obviously they are not obliged to determine and assess their own taxes. Indeed, you will discover that the law specifically requires the Secretary of the Treasury to determine and assess everyone's taxes and then send out bills, just as local governments send out bills for property taxes.

Secret Sections From The Internal Revenue Code

Internal Revenue Code Sections 6201, 6203 and 6303 (Figs. 2-1, 2-2, 2-3) clearly reveal that, according to the law, the federal government is required to levy income taxes in the same manner as local governments levy property taxes. Local governments determine property taxes without demanding assistance from the taxpayer, the taxpayer simply *receives* his bill. Property owners do not pay their property taxes until they receive their tax bills. The law states that the federal government must levy and collect income taxes in precisely the same manner, but the federal government has had more success in keeping this fact secret from the American public than it had in keeping our atomic bomb research secret from the Russians!

Incidentally, state constitutions provide citizens with the same sort of Fifth Amendment protection as does the Federal Constitution, so taxpayers don't have to submit income tax returns to city and state governments either. They, therefore, have to figure out your income taxes (without your help), just like the federal government.

Government Required to Determine and Assess All Taxes

As you can see from Section 6201 (Fig. 2-1), the Secretary of the Treasury is *required* to make the assessments of all taxes "imposed by this title." ("title in this case means Title 26, which is the Internal Revenue Code.) He is required to assess the taxes based upon *his own knowledge*, but, in actuality, he makes his assessment on the basis of the tax returns that the public sends in! Now you know the purpose of a tax return; it is simply to provide the Secretary of the Treasury with information so that he can make his assessment of your taxes which, by law, he is required to do without help from you! Obviously, the Secretary of the Treasury might very well have a problem trying to figure out the taxes for ninety-three million people without their help—but that's his problem, not yours!

---

§ 6201.   Assessment authority.

(a) Authority of Secretary. The Secretary is authorized and required to make the inquiries, determinations, and assessments of all taxes (including interest, additional amounts, additions to the tax, and assessable penalties) imposed by this title, or accruing under any former internal revenue law, which have not been duly paid by stamp at the time and in the manner provided by law. Such authority shall extend to and include the following:

(1) *Taxes shown on return.* The Secretary shall assess all taxes determined by the taxpayer or by the Secretary as to which returns or lists are made under this title.

Figure 2-1
Internal Revenue Code Section 6201

TELLS US THAT THE SEC'TY IS AUTHORIZED & REQ'D. TO MAKE
INQUIRIES, DETERMINATIONS & ASSESSMENT OF ALL TAXES.
HE IS REQUIRED TO ASSESS YOU BEFORE YOU HAVE ANY
TAX LIABILITY AT ALL — PROPERTY TAXES?

Government Required to Record Your Liability

Internal Revenue Code Section 6203 (Fig. 2-2) requires that, after the Secretary of the Treasury determines a citizen's tax liability, he must officially record that liability and, upon the taxpayer's request, furnish him with a copy of that assessment.

It is obvious, then, that the government is required to tell *you* what your tax liability is and not vice versa, as is the case when you tell *them* your liability by sending in a tax return. In addition, it should be clear that the government cannot assess your income tax until all items of income and deductions are in—and that cannot happen until the taxable year closes. So, no one can be officially liable for any taxes at all until the year following the taxable year. Therefore, it logically follows that no one (to the extent that they are even liable for an "income" tax) needs to pay any portion of a 1981 income tax until 1982, any portion of a 1982 income tax until 1983, etc.

Government Required to Bill You for Income Taxes

Section 6303 (Fig. 2-3) of the Internal Revenue Code also requires that, after the Secretary records a citizen's tax liability, he must send a notice, or bill, to each person who is *liable for the tax*; so until you get such a bill, you

---

§ 6203.   Method of assessment.

The assessment shall be made by recording the liability of the taxpayer in the office of the Secretary in accordance with rules or regulations prescribed by the Secretary. Upon request of the taxpayer, the Secretary shall furnish the taxpayer a copy of the record of the assessment.

Figure 2-2
Internal Revenue Code Section 6203

SixTY HAS TO ASSESS YOU WITHOUT YOUR HELP.

are not liable for—and thus are not *required* to pay—any income taxes.

The law on this is so clear that no one should have any trouble understanding it. You don't have to pay taxes until you get a bill!

If you allow taxes to be deducted from your pay, or if you pay estimated taxes, you are paying taxes for which you were never billed and for which you have no liability. Do you usually pay out money before you owe it?

The paying of taxes for which Americans have no legal liability is what the IRS calls "voluntary self-assessment." This means that individuals freely assess themselves for taxes and then volunteer to pay them before any real liability exists. Thus, according to the principle of voluntary self-assessment, Americans make themselves liable for taxes by laying a tax on themselves and then paying the tax which is not legally due. I wonder how many people who borrow money to pay their income taxes know that they are borrowing money to pay taxes that they don't even owe?

So, now you know the real meaning behind "voluntary compliance" and "voluntary self-assessment." They both mean that Americans have no legal obligation to

---

§ 6303. Notice and demand for tax.

(a) **General rule.** Where it is not otherwise provided by this title, the Secretary shall, as soon as practicable, and within 60 days, after the making of an assessment of a tax pursuant to section 6203, give notice to each person liable for the unpaid tax, stating the amount and demanding payment thereof. Such notice shall be left at the dwelling or usual place of business of such person, or shall be sent by mail to such person's last known address.

Figure 2-3
Internal Revenue Code Section 6303

file tax returns or to pay taxes that have never been assessed and for which they have never been billed by the Secretary of the Treasury. How many Americans know this? And, if so few Americans understand this, isn't it about time that the public found out just who has been responsible for keeping them in the dark?

3

The Internal Revenue Code—A Masterpiece of Deception

Government, even in its best state, is but a necessary evil; in its worst state, an intolerable one.

Thomas Paine

The Internal Revenue Code is a thorough fraud. It was deliberately written to mislead the American public concerning federal income taxes. To do this, hundreds of sections had to be written and pieced together in such a way that, while no section technically misstates the law, the sections do, *individually* and *collectively*, convey a meaning that is not actually contained in the law itself.

Consider the following facts. While filing a return is voluntary, the Code makes it *appear* mandatory. While nobody can be liable for taxes until they are assessed, the Code makes it *appear* as though people are automatically liable for taxes as they earn money. While having taxes withheld from your pay is voluntary, the Code makes it *appear* compulsory. While no one has to file and pay estimated income taxes, the Code makes it *appear* that one does. While there cannot be any criminal or civil penalties for not filing an income tax return, the Code makes it *appear* as though criminal and civil penalties do apply. And the list goes on.

The Code is a masterpiece of deception, and, indeed, this section could only be written after hundreds of hours were spent trying to decipher it. We will analyze three sections of the Code to give you some idea of the linguistic gymnastics employed in order to lead taxpayers astray. Sections 6011 and 6012 (Figs. 3-1, & 3-2) are often used by the IRS to mislead Americans into believing that they are required to file tax returns.

Internal Revenue Code Section 6011

This section appears to establish requirements for filing tax returns, since the section is grandiosely entitled "General Requirement of Return, Statement or List." One is led, therefore, to believe that there are, within this section, the "requirements" for filing a tax return, but the section definitley does not establish any such requirements, nor does it require anyone to supply tax information to the government. The section does state that one who is "made liable" (by receiving a bill) for any tax, can, at that time, make either a "return" or a "statement." You have an option. Since filing a tax return is voluntary, the law naturally provides that after receiving your tax bill from the government, you can challenge the assessment! You can do that by either filing an appropriate "statement," taking issue with the assessment, or by filing your own tax "return," claiming a different tax liability.

You could demand in your "statement" that the government furnish you with a complete breakdown of the figures it used in calculating your taxes. This obviously makes more sense than to simply submit, at that time, your own tax return on which you admit to a lesser tax liability, since this could create additional problems for you (see page 52). But, in any case, the law certainly gives you options. You can—

1. file a statement,
2. file a return, or
3. pay the tax bill as rendered.

I would recommend that anybody in this situation file a statement challenging the tax bill as rendered. However, I don't believe that most people would ever face this problem, since I don't believe that they would actually receive a tax bill from the federal government (see page 54).

Of course, the deception in Section 6011 is obvious—no one reading it would have drawn the above information from it. He would have been deliberately (mis)led to believe that the section requires that Americans file income tax returns--when in fact, the section says no such thing.

Internal Revenue Code—Section 6012

This section of the Code is entitled "Persons Re-

---

§ 6011.   General requirement of return, statement, or list.

(a) General rule. When required by regulations prescribed by the Secretary any person <u>made liable</u> for any tax imposed by this title, or for the collection thereof, shall make a <u>return</u> or <u>statement</u> according to the forms and regulations prescribed by the Secretary. Every person required to make a <u>return</u> or <u>statement</u> shall include therein the information required by such forms or regulations.

Figure 3-1
Internal Revenue Code Section 6011

quired to Make Returns of Income," but nowhere in this section does it state that anybody is *required* to file a return. It is important to understand that those who wrote the Code knew that the Code could not *require* anyone to file an income tax return—so many sections of the Code had to be written to sound as though such a requirement existed. Otherwise, who would file? Note that Section 6012 enumerates categories of people who, the section declares, "shall not be required" (Note A). Since no one is "required," what purpose does such a statement serve? Obviously, the statement was phrased in this manner so that the public could draw the erroneous inference that, if some people "are not required" to file, then others *must be* required to file.

Surprise! "Shall" Means "May"

True, this section does state that returns "shall be made" (Note B) by various individuals, but "shall," as used here, does not mean "mandatory" in the legal sense.

---

§ 6012. Persons required to make returns of income.

    (a) **General rule.** Returns with respect to income taxes under subtitle A } C
B——▸shall be made by the following:
      (1)(A) Every individual having for the taxable year a gross income of $1,000 or more, except that a return shall not be required of an individual (other than an individual described in subparagraph (c))—
         (i) who is not married (determined by applying section 143), is not A a surviving spouse (as defined in section 2(a)), and for the taxable year has a gross income of less than $3,300,
         (ii) who is a surviving spouse (as so defined) and for the taxable year has a gross income of less than $4,400, or
         (iii) who is entitled to make a joint return under section 6013 and whose gross income, when combined with the gross income of his spouse, is, for the taxable year, less than $5,400, but only if such individual and his spouse, at the close of the taxable year, had the same household as their home.

Figure 3–2
Internal Revenue Code Section 6012

A key to understanding the government's success in misleading the public regarding income taxes involves the Code's use of the words "shall" and "must" in place of the word "required." The public naturally believes that the words "shall" and "must" in a statute, operate as a command—but when these words are applied to the public in connection with federal statutes, the words take on a different meaning. Here are three court decisions that explain this principle:

The word "shall" in a statute may be construed to mean "may," particularly in order to avoid a constitutional doubt.[1]

If necessary, to avoid unconstitutionality of a statute, "shall" will be deemed equivalent to "may."[2]

"Shall" in a statute may be construed to mean "may" in order to avoid constitutional doubt.[3]

So it is clear that the word "shall," when used in statutes, means "may," especially when the constitutionality of a statute is at stake. Clearly then, this construction must be used throughout the Internal Revenue Code in order to preserve its constitutionality. In terms of Section 6012, if "shall" is construed to be *mandatory*, it would cause the entire Code to be unconstitutional, since the Code would then be in irreconcilable conflict with the Fifth Amendment. Therefore, the word "shall" cannot be construed as meaning "mandatory," in this case, but

1. *Fort Howard Paper Co.* v. *Fox River Heights Sanitary Dist*
2. *Gow* v. *Consolidated Coppermines Corp*
3. *George Williams College* v. *Village of Williams Bay*

must be interpreted as "may," according to the principle cited in the three cases mentioned above.

In addition to the above, the United States Supreme Court held:

> As against the government, the word "shall" when used in statutes is to be construed as "may," unless a contrary intention is manifest.[4]

Therefore, even the Supreme Court has ruled that the word "shall," as used in the Internal Revenue Code, must be construed as "may," since no other intention is "manifest" or even possible.

A United States Court of Appeals, in the case of *Ballou* v. *Kemp*, gives significant added insight as to how we can determine when "shall" in a statute really means "may."

> The word "shall" in a statute may be construed as "may" where the connection in which it is used or the relation to which it is put with other parts of the same statute indicates that the legislature intended that it should receive such a construction.

Since Section 6012 does state that some citizens are "not required" to file, if it were the legislative intent of the statute to declare that others *were* "required" to file, then the section would have read (Note C):

> Returns with respect to income taxes under Subtitle A *are required* to be made by the following . . .

Since such wording does *not* appear, it is therefore obvious that the legislature did not intend to convey a *mandatory construction*. Again, we see that "shall" should be interpreted in this section as "may."

4. *Cairo and Fulton R. R. Co.* v. *Hecht*

It is also clear that the section uses the two terms "shall" and "not required" to imply that some persons *are required to file*, because others are not (which, of course the section does *not* say). That the deception was deliberate cannot be seriously questioned, as the Court of Appeals also observed in the previously quoted Ballou case:

> It can hardly be called accidental that Congress used mandatory language in one part of the chapter [law] and permissive in another.

Section 6020—The Key to Many Code Mysteries

While you already *know* that nobody is required to file a tax return, Code Section 6020 (Fig. 3–3) is where the law actually says it. It also provides an important key that helps explain some of the Code's puzzling language. Note that provision b of that section states that the

NOT REQ'D BY TITLE.

---

§ 6020.   Returns prepared for or executed by Secretary.

(a) Preparation of return by Secretary. If any person <u>shall fail to make a</u>
A → <u>return required by this title or by regulations prescribed thereunder,</u> but
shall <u>consent</u> to disclose all information necessary for the preparation
B → thereof, then, and in that case, the Secretary may prepare such return,
which, being signed by such person, may be received by the Secretary as
the return of such person.

(b) Execution of return by Secretary.

(1) Authority of Secretary to execute return. <u>If any person fails to make</u>
<u>any return</u> (other than a declaration of estimated tax required under
section 6015) required by an internal revenue law or regulation made
thereunder at the time prescribed therefor, or makes, willfully or
otherwise, a false or fraudulent return, <u>the Secretary shall make such</u>
<u>return from his own knowledge</u> and from such information as he can
obtain through testimony or otherwise.

Figure 3–3
Internal Revenue Code Section 6020

**The Section that Establishes that
filing a Return is Voluntary**

IF YOU DON'T CONSENT, HE HAS TO PREPARE IT HIMSELF.

Secretary shall make a return for anyone who doesn't voluntarily make one and that the Secretary shall prepare it " . . . from his own knowledge and from such information as he can obtain through testimony or otherwise." This is the only place in the entire Internal Revenue Code where someone is clearly directed to prepare a tax return. Please note that the one directed to prepare it is the Secretary of the Treasury, not a private citizen. So whenever the Code uses such language as "when required" to file a return, it is the Secretary of the Treasury that the Code refers to, not private citizens. Citizens, of course, wouldn't know this and, seeing such language, assume it refers to them, rather than to the Secretary.

A perfect example of this very kind of subterfuge blatantly occurs within Section 6020 itself. By what logic can this section speak of persons who ". . . fail to make a return required by this title or by regulations prescribed thereunder" (see Note A), when the seciton itself declares that citizens must *"consent"* (see Note B) to disclose information before the Secretary can prepare returns for them, while, if they don't consent, the Secretary shall make the return "from his own knowledge." Thus, Section 6020 establishes all by itself that no citizen is required in *any* circumstance to file a tax return. It therefore strains one's credulity to see how this section could even have suggested that anyone is "required" to file tax returns! If anyone is said to be "required," it must be the Secretary of the Treasury, since he is required to make a return, either with a citizen's help, as provided in paragraph *a*, or without it, as provided in paragraph *b*!

Thus, Section 6020 provides irrefutable proof that, according to the Code, citizens are simply not required to file income tax returns. If any section of the Code suggests otherwise, then it must have been written to mislead. And we can see how resourceful the government is at misleading!

4

How the IRS Violates the Law

Let us refer once again to the Privacy Act Notice (Fig. 4-1). The notice made its first appearance in a 1040 Booklet in 1976, following the passage of Public Law 93-579, which required that all federal agencies—

... inform each individual whom it asks to supply information ...

(A) the authority . . . which authorizes the solicitation of the information and whether disclosure of such information is *mandatory* or *voluntary*;
(B) the principal purpose or purposes for which the information is intended to be used;
(C) the routine uses which may be made of the information;
(D) the effects on him, *if any,* of not providing all or any part of the requested information.[1] (emphasis added)

---

1. 5 USC Section 552a, Sec. 3, par. (e)(3)

41

Privacy Act Notice

The Privacy Act of 1974 says that each Federal agency that asks you for information must tell you:

a. Its legal right to ask for the information and whether the law says you must give it.

b. What major purposes the agency has in asking for it, and how it will be used.

c. What could happen if the agency does not receive it.

For the Internal Revenue Service, the law covers:

● Tax returns and any papers filed with them.

● Any questions we need to ask you so we can:

Complete, correct, or process your return.

Figure your tax.

Collect tax, interest, or penalties.

Our legal right to ask for information is Internal Revenue Code sections 6001 and 6011 and their regulations. They say that you must file a return or statement with us for any tax you are liable for. Code section 6109 and its regulations say that you must show your social security number on what you file. This is so we know who you are, and can process your return and papers.

You must fill in all parts of the tax form that apply to you. But you do not have to check the boxes for the Presidential Election Campaign Fund.

We ask for tax return information to carry out the Internal Revenue laws of the United States. We need it to figure and collect the right amount of tax.

We may give the information to the Department of Justice and to other Federal agencies, as provided by law. We may also give it to States, the District of Columbia, and U.S. commonwealths or possessions to carry out their tax laws. And we may give it to foreign governments because of tax treaties they have with the United States.

If a return is not filed, or if we don't receive the information we ask for, the law provides that a penalty may be charged. And we may have to disallow the exemptions, exclusions, credits, deductions, or adjustments shown on the tax return. This could make the tax higher or delay any refund. Interest may also be charged.

Please keep this notice with your records. It may help you if we ask you for other information.

If you have questions about the rules for filing and giving information, please call or visit any Internal Revenue Service office.

This is the only notice we must give you to explain the Privacy Act. However, we may give you other notices if we have to examine your return or collect any tax, interest, or penalties.

Not True!

Not True!

A

B

C

D

Figure 4-1

Privacy Act Notice–Internal Revenue

SELECTIVE SERVICE SYSTEM
PRIVACY ACT STATEMENT

A The Military Selective Service Act, Selective Service Regulations, and the President's Proclamation on Registration require that you provide the indicated information, including your Social Security Account Number.

The principal purpose of the required information is to establish your registration with the Selective Service System. This information may be furnished to the following agencies for the purposes stated:

Department of Defense—for exchange of information concerning registration, classification, enlistment, examination and induction of individuals, availability of Standby Reservists, and if Block 8 is checked, identification of prospects for recruiting.

Alternate service employers—for exchange of information with employers regarding a registrant who is a conscientious objector for the purpose of placement and supervision of performance of alternate service in lieu of induction into military service.

Department of Justice—for review and processing of suspected violations of the Military Selective Service Act, or for perjury, and for defense of a civil action arising from administrative processing under such Act.

Federal Bureau of Investigation—for location of an individual when suspected of violation of the Military Selective Service Act.

Immigration and Naturalization Service—to provide information for use in determining an individual's eligibility for re-entry into the United States.

Department of State—for determination of an alien's eligibility for possible entry into the United States and United States citizenship.

Office of Veterans' Reemployment Rights, United States Department of Labor—to assist veterans in need of information concerning reemployment rights.

B General Public—Registrant's Name, Selective Service Number, Date of Birth and Classification, Military Selective Service Act Section 6, 50 U.S.C. App. 456.

Your failure to provide the required information may violate the Military Selective Service Act. Conviction of such violation may result in imprisonment for not more than five years or a fine of not more than $10,000 or both imprisonment and fine.

Figure 4-2
Privacy Act Statement-Selective Service

So, according to the law, the IRS Privacy Act Notice is supposed to tell you whether filing a return is "mandatory or voluntary." What could be simpler?

Read through the Privacy Act Notice and see if it specifically tells you *anywhere* whether filing a tax return is "mandatory or voluntary." It doesn't! Thus, the IRS Privacy Act Notice is in clear violation of the law. This becomes readily apparent if we check the IRS Privacy Act Notice against the one used in connection with the Selective Service Act (Fig. 4–2). That notice clearly tells the reader (at both A and B) that the information being asked for is *required*.

In addition, according to the law, the notice is supposed to tell you what the consequences of not filing might be, "if any." The law is very specific on this. If you can be fined or sent to jail for not filing a tax return, then, according to the law, the IRS is required to tell you that in its Privacy Act Notice.

So, look through the Privacy Act Notice and see if it notifies you *anywhere* that if you don't file a tax return, you may be fined or sent to prison. It does not. Compare this aspect of the IRS Notice again with the Selective Service Statement, which indicates very clearly (at Note B)—

> Your failure to provide the required information may violate the military Selective Service Act. Conviction of such a violation may result in imprisonment for not more than 5 years or a fine of not more that $10,000 or both imprisonment and fine.

Thus, it is obvious that if Americans could legally be fined and sent to prison for not filing a return, by law, that fact *would have to be stated in the IRS Privacy Act Notice in the same manner as such information appears in the Selective Service Privacy Act Statement.* Such a statement does not appear, however, and since American citizens actually have been fined and imprisoned for not filing tax returns, one of two possibilities must exist:

1. the Privacy Act Notice is so woefully incomplete in this matter as to suggest criminal culpability on the part of those government officials who prepared it, or
2. the Privacy Act Notice *is* complete—which would mean that there are Americans who have been *illegally* fined and imprisoned for not filing tax returns. (And so, federal judges and U.S. attorneys have been prosecuting and sentencing Americans illegally.)

This means that, at the very least, either IRS officials are breaking the law, or federal judges and U.S. attorneys are breaking the law.

In reality, all of them are breaking the law. Let me explain. First of all, the IRS Privacy Act Notice is *incomplete* in the sense that it does not tell you whether sending in a tax return is "voluntary" or "mandatory," which it is required to do by law. It is *complete,* however, as far as not stating that failure to file a return may be punishable by fine or imprisonment. We know this from the material already covered in this book, so it is not surprising that the Privacy Act does not allege any such thing. What is interesting, though, is the notice's attempt to imply legal consequences by its use of the word "penalty" and its reference to "interest charges." Remember, if being fined or imprisoned could be a consequence of not filing a return, then the Privacy Act Notice is legally required to advise you of that.

Since no criminal penalties are indicated in the IRS Privacy Act Notice, you can treat this as the government's *legal notice* to you that there are no criminal penalties connected with not filing a tax return. Therefore, if you stop filing tax returns because of that legal notice, the government is barred from prosecuting you, since you have, in good faith, relied on their very own notice.

The Selective Service Privacy Act Statement, on the other hand, clearly puts those who don't supply the required information *on notice* that they risk fines and imprisonment. The absence of a comparable warning on the IRS Privacy Act Notice is, in fact, notice to you by the federal government that you do not risk such penalties for not filing.

You ask, "How can you say that, when Americans have been criminally prosecuted, fined and imprisoned for not filing?" The answer is that those people either could not, or did not, use the Privacy Act Notice properly (see page 130).

Remember, the issue here is not to explain the law. You already know that the law doesn't require you to file tax returns. Our purpose in explaining the Privacy Act Notice is (1) to give you a clear picture of the lengths to which the IRS will go in order to mislead the public concerning income taxes; (2) to prove conclusively that federal courts are conducting criminal trials that federal officials know are illegal; and (3) to gain an understanding of how the Privacy Act Notice can be used procedurally at an arraignment, should a federal judge ever attempt to prosecute you illegally for the "crime" of not filing a tax return. In other words, law-abiding Americans simply have to learn extraordinary techniques in order to combat the lawlessness that exists in federal courts on matters relating to income taxes.

The Privacy Act Notice establishes beyond question that illegal prosecutions have been taking place in America. If citizens could legally be fined and jailed for not filing tax returns, the Privacy Act Notice would have had to say so. The absence of such a warning proves that there is no legal justification for these prosecutions! The fact that U.S. attorneys and judges have sent people to jail for not filing, simply proves that in those courtrooms the real criminals were not those on trial.

Proof That You Can't Trust the IRS— The Privacy Act Notice

The Privacy Act Notice could have been a very simple and clear statement, as is the Selective Service Privacy Act Notice Statement. But the one that appears in the 1040 Booklet is needlessly long, complicated, and confusing and doesn't seem to give the reader the information required by the Act. First of all, in explaining the requirements of the Privacy Act itself, the notice says, "... each federal agency that asks you for information must tell you ... whether the law says *you must give it*" (Note A). That, of course, is not true. Rather, the law specifically says that the federal agency must tell you whether supplying the requested information is "mandatory" or "voluntary." Consider, therefore, the magnitude of the deceit—if not the actual violation of the law— that is evident here. Not only doesn't the Privacy Act Notice notify citizens that giving the information is *voluntary,*which under the law it was duty bound to do, but the notice actually attempts to convince them of the opposite—that giving the information is *mandatory.* Talk about *chutzpa!*

The IRS notice was written in such a confusing and complicated manner because the IRS did not want to admit to American taxpayers that filing a return is "voluntary" (as the law required them to do), and because the IRS couldn't legally say that filing is "mandatory." Therefore, the notice had to be designed so that—

1. the public would be made to believe that filing is mandatory while,
2. for legal purposes, the IRS would escape the responsibility of actually stating that filing is mandatory.

Let us examine how the IRS sought to achieve both objectives.

How the Privacy Act Notice Convinces Taxpayers that Filing is Mandatory

The law states that each agency asking for information must tell the person asked whether giving the information is mandatory or voluntary. This is clearly done in the Selective Service Privacy Act Statement. Note, however, the technique used by the IRS to get itself off the legal hook of having to commit itself as to whether filing is mandatory or not. It refers the reader to two Internal Revenue Code sections (Note B)—as if every taxpayer had a copy of the Code in his living room for easy reference—and states that it is *these sections* that say " that you must file a tax return."

In this way, the IRS tries to escape taking any position itself! The extent of the subterfuge in this ploy is evident. First of all the statement itself is false, because neither section says that anybody "must" file a tax return. (As a matter of fact, the word *must* doesn't even appear!) We have already covered Section 6011, so Section 6001 is reproduced in full (Fig 4-3) for your perusal. You can see for yourself that neither section says that anybody "must file a return." Obviously, though, citizens reading that statement in the Privacy Act Notice (and naively assuming that official government announcements are truthful)[2] will conclude that filing a return is mandatory, regardless of any other language appearing in the notice.

The IRS, of course, recognizes that taxpayers will interpret the phrase "must file a return" as being mandatory. But even if the Code sections cited said this, filing would still not be mandatory. Why? Because "must" in that context legally means "may." IRS officials knew this, of course, so they felt that they could use "must" without *technically* violating any laws.

---

§ 6001. Notice or regulations requiring records, statements, and special returns.

Every person liable for any tax imposed by this title, or for the collection thereof, shall keep such records, render such statements, make such returns, and comply with such rules and regulations as the Secretary from time to time prescribe. Whenever in the judgment of the Secretary it is necessary, he may require any person, by notice served upon such person or by regulations, to make such returns, render such statements, or keep such records, as the Secretary deems sufficient to show whether or not such person is liable for tax under this title. The only records which an employer shall be required to keep under this section in connection with charged tips shall be charge receipts and copies of statements furnished by employees under section 6053(a).

Figure 4-3
Internal Revenue Code Section 6001

2. See *The Biggest Con*, chapters 3 & 4, regarding false government representations of the National Debt (which is officially underreported by some 95%) and on the financial condition of Social Security.

"Must" as Used in the Privacy Act Notice
Legally Means "May"

I have already explained why "shall" must legally be interpreted as meaning "may" when the word is directed at the public in connection with the filing of income tax returns. The same legal principle applies to "must," but the general public is completely unaware of this. Here are a few excerpts from court cases to illustrate:

> Words like "may," "must," "shall," etc., are constantly used in statutes without intending that they be taken literally.[3]

> "Must" as used in statutes has been frequently construed not to be mandatory.[4]

Obviously, "must" is used to (mis)lead taxpayers to believe that filing tax returns is mandatory.

The Privacy Act Notice Makes Fraudulent
Claims

Note that the Privacy Act states that "if a return is not filed or if we don't receive the information we ask for, the law provides that a penalty may be charged" (Note C). Well, that statement is completely false, since there are simply *no penalties* for not filing a return. If there were such penalties, then filing a return would be based on compulsory compliance, not voluntary. The Code, interestingly enough, provides penalties for *late* filing, but there are no penalties for *not filing at all!* This should be clear from the material we have already covered, so this statement will give you some idea of the extent to which the IRS will go in order to mislead the public on the issue of taxes. The Selective Service Statement speci-

3. *Fields* v. *United States*

4. *Brinkley* v. *Brinkley*

fically uses such words as "fine" and "imprisonment," but it does not use the word "penalty." However, I am sure that many who read the IRS Privacy Act Notice interpreted the word "penalty" as meaning "fine or imprisonment" or both, which is not the case (but which is obviously the interpretation that the IRS is trying to convey.)

So, by deliberately avoiding making a clear statement concerning whether filing a return is mandatory or voluntary, by deliberately making misstatements and misleading references to specific Code sections, by conveying an erroneous legal meaning through the word "must," and by making reference to nonexistent penalties and interest charges, the Privacy Act Notice attempts to convince the public that filing a return is mandatory—the exact opposite of the truth. Thus, the Privacy Act Notice deliberately subverts the very purpose for its appearance in a 1040 Booklet.

Amazingly, the IRS Privacy Act Notice actually violates the regulations of the Treasury Department— the very department in which the IRS operates. These regulations (Fig. 4-4) not only require that the notice

Figure 4-4

> (2) To insure that the form or a separate form that can be retained by the individual <u>makes clear to the individual which information he is required</u> by law to disclose and the authority for that requirement and <u>which information is voluntary;</u>
>
> (4) To insure that the form or a separate form that can be retained by the individual <u>clearly indicates to the individual the effect in terms of rights, benefits or privileges of not</u> providing all or part of the requested information; and

Code of Federal Regulations
Title 31, Section 1.35

"make clear to the individual" which information is required and which is voluntary, but that it also "clearly indicate to the individual the effect in terms of rights, benefits, or privileges of not providing all or part of the requested information." Therefore, in both cases the law *and* the Treasury regulations were violated. Since there are many benefits of not filing (no information that can be used against you is given to the government, no assessment will have been made yet, you cannot be subject to fraud or late filing penalties, etc.), the IRS was required to inform you of many of the things that you are learning for the first time from this book.

How the IRS Attempts to Stay "Technically" Within the Law

Despite the IRS's obvious attempt to make the Privacy Act Notice sound as though filing a return is mandatory, its language (if one understands how to interpret it) confirms that filing a return is voluntary. First of all, the notice says that you "must" file a "return" *or* "statement" for any tax that you are "liable for" (Note B). Since we know that "must" legally means "may" in this context, the Privacy Act Notice is legally saying that, after you get your tax bill (after you are made "liable" for a tax) you "may" at that time file a "statement" challenging the tax bill, or you "may" file a "return" showing your own calculations. Obviously, another option is to pay the tax for which you have been made liable. So, this section of the Privacy Act Notice merely confirms what we already knew from our analysis of Section 6011.

Another section of the Privacy Act Notice covertly informs the reader that filing a tax return is voluntary (Note C). Notice that the paragraph begins, "If a return is not filed or if we don't receive the information ... we may have to disallow the exemptions, exclusions, credits, deductions or adjustments shown *on the tax return.*" What tax return are they talking about? Remember, this paragraph refers to cases in which "a return is not filed"! They must, then, be referring to the return that the government is supposed to compute for you if you don't voluntarily submit one! This is confirmed in the next sentence with the statement, "This could make the tax higher or delay any refunds."

Here the Privacy Act Notice admits that taxpayers may be eligible for refunds even though they filed no tax returns! Who, then, computed the refunds? The notice goes on to say that "interest may also be charged." This is a false statement. The Code simply does not provide interest charges for not filing a tax return; though it does provide that interest can be charged for late filing or for nonpayment of an assessed tax. But there are no interest penalties for not filing a tax return at all.

In reality, the Privacy Act Notice is saying (but in language that even a Philadelphia lawyer couldn't penetrate) that if taxpayers voluntarily prepare their returns, they would probably calculate a lower tax than the government would, since taxpayers would take advantage of all exemptions, exclusions and deducations, while the government would not. As I have said before, if the government calculated a higher tax than the taxpayer thinks he is liable for, the taxpayer can always challenge the government's assessment and claim a lower tax. If this is true, then why not let the government calculate your tax, as the Privacy Act Notice tells you it will?

What is the Likelihood of the IRS Calculating Your Tax?

I suggest that it is practically impossible for the Secretary of the Treasury to make a correct assessment if taxpayers give him no information. His job, neverthe-

less, is to make a correct assessment, and there is nothing
in the law that says that you have to help him. You could,
for example, prepare your usual return, but instead of
sending it in, keep it on file with your supporting documentation to see if the tax bill you eventually receive
(who knows how many years that will take) coincides
with your own calculations. If it doesn't, you can use that
return, with your other documentation, to challenge the
Secretary's calculations.

Imagine the impact this would have if the friends of
a nonfiler saw him pay no more in taxes when the IRS
assessed him years later. They would all immediately
stop filing, too, and wait for the IRS to assess them as
well. The practice would spread like wildfire. To prevent
this from happening, I suggest that the IRS largely ignores nonfilers for three reasons:

1. They are simply too difficult to locate.
2. Even if they can be located, it is too time-
   consuming and difficult to try to determine the
   tax of an uncooperative, nonfiling citizen.
3. They would just as soon have the public believe
   that nonfilers are "lucky," and that it is only a
   matter of time before they "get caught."

Of course, the IRS has no choice in the matter since
there is no way that they can possibly calculate the
correct tax liability of even a small fraction of the American public. Also, since business and financial institu-
tions send wage, dividend and interest information to the
IRS, the public thinks that Big Brother really knows how
much everyone is earning—but that is just so much
hogwash!

On April 15, 1977, the *Wall Street Journal* reported

in a front-page article that most of the "hundreds of
millions of documents" concerning dividends and other
payments that apply to individual taxpayers (and "all"
of the documents relating to corporations) "are destroyed
before anybody even looks at them! This year the IRS
will shred, pulverize and burn about 250 million unexam-
ined documents submitted by business." It also reported
that the IRS was buying eleven new pulverizing ma-
chines, costing $80,000 each, "to help destroy the docu-
ments." Just consider what all this needless waste is
costing American working-consumers, since it is they, in
the final analysis, who will have to bear the cost, either in
terms of lower wages or higher prices.

The inability of the IRS to assess significant
numbers of Americans was openly admitted by Roscoe
Egger, Jr., the current IRS Commissioner, in an interview reported in the April 20, 1980, issue of *U.S. News &
World Report*, when replying to the question, "What
would happen if millions of people got sore and refused to
report their income voluntarily?" He stated, "If taxpayers in those numbers refused, the system simply wouldn't
work." So, American taxpayers shouldn't complain
about being fleeced by the federal government, since they
can stop the fleecing any time they want.

The Government's Initial Response to Nonfilers

Many people believe that if they stop filing tax returns IRS storm troopers will come knocking at their
door the moment they find out. This will not happen. If
the IRS does anything at all, they will send you (perhaps,
in a year or two) a form letter (see Figs. 4-5, 4-6). Note
that the letter I received inquiring about my 1979 tax
return was not sent to me until August 14, 1981, and I

PART II

I DID NOT FILE THE FORM BECAUSE (CHECK APPLICABLE BLOCKS):

☐ Income was less than the amount required for filing. (Please explain below, under "Remarks".)

☐ Business was closed on (Date) _____
I had no employees during the period shown, but I expect to pay taxable wages in the future. (Give date, if known. _____)

☐ I am no longer liable for filing this form. (Please explain below, under "Remarks".)

☒ Other. (Please explain below, under "Remarks".)
NOTE: You should file a return to get a refund of any prepaid tax, refundable credits, or tax withheld.

EXPLANATION OF PENALTY CHARGES

The penalty for filing late is 5 percent a month (or part of a month) on any tax that is unpaid by the due date of the return, up to a maximum penalty of 25 percent of the unpaid tax.

The penalty for filing late or filing an incomplete Form 1065, U.S. Partnership Return of Income, is $50 times the number of partners in the partnership during any part of the tax year. The penalty is charged for each month or part of a month the return is late or incomplete, up to a maximum of 5 months.

The penalty for late payment of tax is computed from the due date of the return at ½ of 1 percent of the unpaid tax for each month or part of the month the tax remains unpaid. It cannot exceed 25 percent of the unpaid amount.

If both the late filing and late payment penalties apply for any month, the combination of the two is limited to 5 percent of the unpaid tax for that month.

The penalty rates for underpayment of estimated tax are shown on the enclosed Notice 394.

The penalty for late deposits is 5 percent of the amount of underpayment without regard to the time the underpayment continues. (This penalty does not apply to income tax returns.)

In addition to the penalties described above, exempt organizations may be liable for a penalty of $10 a day for each day the required form is late and managers of private foundations may be liable for a penalty of $10 a day for each day the annual report of a private foundation is late.

Remarks: I am not required to file, see USC 26 Section 6020; also see Flora v. US 362 US 145, 176.

Signature	Title (business tax returns)	Telephone (with area code) Home: Business:	Date

Form 4902 (Rev. 6-80)

Figure 4-5

Department of the Treasury
Internal Revenue Service

Request for Information about Tax Form

08-14-81

Identifying Number		
047-16-2491	SCHI XJ	
30 7912	8131 608	
06-01		8131
SEL 28	ND	1 PC
AG 51	WH	0 DY79
OT		PYNC-8
AGR		
IRP	18000	COPYS-A595
CB	.00	2
AGI	0 EX	0
NT	0 TDA CD	
DF		LRF 73
FS 1		SSA

IRWIN A SCHIFF
2405 WHITNEY AVE   4901
HAMDEN, CT   06518

If address is not correct, please change

Dear Taxpayer:

We have no record of receiving your Form   1040
US INDIVIDUAL INCOME TAX RETURN   for the period ended
12-31-79

Please complete Part I of this letter and return it to us if you FILED the form.
Please complete Part II of this letter and return it to us if you are NOT REQUIRED TO FILE for the period in question.

If you ARE LIABLE for filing the form, but HAVE NOT YET FILED, please do so within the next 2 weeks. Attach this letter to the form and include payment for any tax due plus interest and penalty as provided by law. (See enclosed Notice 394.) Unless you had reasonable cause for delay, you may also be liable for the penalties described on the back of this letter. If you believe you had reasonable cause for filing late and for paying late (other than estimated tax), please explain under "Remarks". Otherwise, include any penalties with your payment.

You may disregard this letter if you filed within the last week and used the name and identifying number shown above. If we find we need additional information to locate the form, we will contact you again.

We have enclosed an envelope for your use. Thank you for your cooperation.

Sincerely yours,

Harry L Thurston
Chief, Collection Branch

Enclosures:
Notice 394
Envelope

PART I

Please enter information exactly as shown on the tax form you filed

Name and address on tax form

Employer identification number (business tax returns).
Social security number (individual tax returns). If filed jointly, show both numbers.
Yours
Spouse's

Date filed	Tax year/period on form	Form number	If paid by check, enter endorsement date and number stamped on check

Please complete the signature area on the back of this letter.   Form 4901 (Rev. 6-80)

INTERNAL REVENUE SERVICE 4901
SC COLLECTION BRANCH
P.O. BOX 6000   DY79 PYNC-8
ANDOVER, MA 01899   047-16-2491 SCHI 30 7912 28
        0 18000 .00

Figure 4-6

have never received any letters from the IRS concerning the tax returns that I didn't file for the years 1977, 1978, 1980. Notice that the reasons given for not filing a return on Part II (Fig. 4-5) do not apply. Notice also how the form tries to mislead and intimidate citizens by the use of such expressions as "if you are NOT REQUIRED TO FILE," and, "if you ARE LIABLE for filing the form, but HAVE NOT YET FILED." You should now be able to see through such IRS language.

In the EXPLANATION OF PENALTY CHARGES, you can see that the only penalties indicated are those for "filing late," for filing returns that are "late or incomplete," for taxes that are "unpaid," or for the "underpayment" of estimated taxes.

Penalties indicated for "unpaid" taxes and "underpayment" of taxes do not apply to those who don't file, since those who haven't filed *owe no taxes*; they have not assessed themselves, nor have they been assessed by the Secretary.

If you get such a letter, you can reply to it in the manner indicated in the "remarks" section (Fig. 4-5) and I doubt that you will ever hear from the IRS again on this matter. The IRS, however, may still attempt to assess you, but I doubt it.

*Purposes for which the Government Uses
Return Information*

The Privacy Act Notice is also required to tell you the purposes for which the government agency may use the requested information. Most Americans naturally assume that the only purpose for tax information on a 1040 is to show the government how they calculated their taxes. There are, however, other purposes for which the government uses this information. This can be found on the Privacy Act Notice (Note D). The government tells you, "We may give the information to the Department of Justice and other agencies as provided by law."

We had, of course, commented earlier that the government certainly cannot "require" Americans to give private, personal and financial information to the Department of Justice for use against themselves. But, if the Department of Justice cannot demand such information from citizens directly, can it get it from them indirectly by having the government require that citizens first give the information to the IRS? Of course not. Notice, though, all the other government agencies, both federal and state, that have access to return information. (Section 6103 of the Code lists numerous government agencies and departments to which your return can be given.)

It should be obvious that the only reason these other agencies would want your tax return is to be able to use the information in it against you. Why would you voluntarily give all of that personal financial data to the IRS, since it could be turned over to these other agencies? Note, also, that such information can be given to "foreign governments"! What constitutional authority, one might ask, does the federal government have that would permit it to act as an international conveyor belt, supplying personal and financial data about Americans to foreign governments? None whatsoever! Obviously, since Americans cannot be required to turn over such information to foreign governments, they can only be tricked into doing it by the IRS!

In Summation

So, the IRS is required *by law* to tell taxpayers whether filing an income tax return is voluntary or man-

datory. The Privacy Act Notice does neither! It avoids the
legal requirements by referring readers to two Code sections which it deliberately misrepresents. Also, the notice erroneously implies that penalties and interest
charges can be levied against those who file no tax returns at all. Thus, the IRS Privacy Act Notice in no way
complies with the provision of Public Law 93-579. The
IRS's deliberate attempt to evade the legal responsibility
imposed upon it by Public Law 93-579 indicates criminal
culpability on the part of IRS officials. Since the IRS is
responsible for the prosecution of private citizens who, it
contends, violate our tax laws, should not IRS officials be
similarly prosecuted for their blatant violations of Public
Law 93-579?

When everything is said and done, the Privacy Act
Notice confirms the information in the first three chapters of this book, which is that:

1. the filing of a tax return is voluntary, and
2. after being made liable for a tax (that is, after you
   get your tax bill) you can, *if you wish*, file a statement, file a return, or pay the tax bill as rendered.

In any case, there is nothing in the Privacy Act Notice
that tells you that you are *required* to file a tax return or
that you risk criminal prosecution, fines, or jail for failing
to file a tax return.

5

How To Stop Paying Income Taxes

> By means which the law permits, a taxpayer has the right to decrease the amount of what otherwise would be his taxes, or altogether to avoid them.
>
> United States Supreme Court
> *Gregory* v. *Helvering* (1934)

If you are self-employed, retired, or simply living on income from dividends, interest, rent, alimony, etc., it is easy to stop paying income taxes. Just stop! On the basis of the material in the first four chapters of this book, you should know that you do not have to file an estimated tax return or pay quarterly tax estimates and that, as long as you have not been officially assessed or notified by the government that you owe any taxes, you don't have to pay the government a penny.

If you are an employee, taxes are probably being withheld from your wages—but only because *you* authorized it. To prevent such withholding, you need merely withdraw that authorization. You, of course, did not realize that, along with voluntarily filing tax returns, you had authorized the withholding of taxes that you didn't owe, based on the principle of self-assessment. To stop the withholding of taxes from your pay, you have to stop assessing yourself. Wait for the Secretary to assess you; that is his job. Remember, if neither you nor the Secretary assess you for any taxes, you can't possibly owe any; therefore, no taxes can be legally withheld from your pay.

How to Stop Your Employer From Withholding Taxes From Your Pay

Most employees, on the W-4 Form (Fig. 5–1) they are asked to complete when first hired, unwittingly indicate on line 1 the number of tax exemptions they have. A single person, for instance, would normally write *1* in the space provided, while a married individual with three dependents would write in *4*.

The deception perpetrated by the government in this situation should now be obvious. The government relies on workers to incorrectly assume that they incur a tax liability by the mere receipt of wages. Employees have been led to believe that they incur a tax liability the moment they get paid and, therefore, think they have to have taxes deducted from their wages as they are paid. This is not true! No employee can have a tax liability until his taxes are officially assessed and a bill is sent to him. If a worker has not received a bill for taxes, he has no tax liability.

If employees, nevertheless, freely choose to assess themselves and pay taxes they don't owe, then they can't be said to have been coerced, and taxes collected in this manner would truly have been collected on the basis of *self-assessment*.

Form **W-4**
(Rev. October 1979)

Department of the Treasury—Internal Revenue Service

Employee's Withholding Allowance Certificate

Print your full name ▶ IMA FREEMAN   Your social security number ▶ 001 : 02 : 0003

Address (including ZIP code) ▶ 25 HALLELUJAH DRIVE, LIBERTYVILLE, U.S.A. 00511

Marital status: ☒ Single   ☐ Married   ☐ Married, but withhold at higher Single rate

Note: If married, but legally separated, or spouse is a nonresident alien, check the single block.

1 Total number of allowances you are claiming (from line F of the worksheet on page 2) . . . .

2 Additional amount, if any, you want deducted from each pay (if your employer agrees) . . . . $

3 I claim exemption from withholding because (see instructions and check boxes below that apply):

   a ☒ Last year I did not owe any Federal income tax and had a right to a full refund of ALL income tax withheld, AND

   b ☒ This year I do not expect to owe any Federal income tax and expect to have a right to a full refund of ALL income tax withheld. If both

    a and b apply, enter "EXEMPT" here ▶   EXEMPT ◀——A

   c If you entered "EXEMPT" on line 3b, are you a full-time student? . . . . ☐ Yes ☒ No

Under the penalties of perjury, I certify that I am entitled to the number of withholding allowances claimed on this certificate, or if claiming exemption from withholding, that I am entitled to claim the exempt status.

Employee's signature ▶ Ima Freeman   Date ▶ JANUARY 15 , 19 82

Employer's name and address (including ZIP code) (FOR EMPLOYER'S USE ONLY)   Employer identification number

Figure 5-1

Surprisingly, such a *choice* is actually given to employees on a W-4—only they don't know it, because the IRS has taken extraordinary and illegal measures to hide it from them.

Note that the form (Note A) does provide that employees can claim "EXEMPT" from withholding. By not claiming "EXEMPT," employees *voluntarily* agree to pay a tax that they don't owe, thereby signaling their willingness to assess themselves. The government must provide this choice, or they cannot even claim that the withholding of taxes is based on self-assessment. If there were no choice, the withholding of taxes would, by law, be based on distraint.

It is important to understand the meaning of the word *distraint* in order to understand the transparent illegality of the IRS's attempt to intimidate employees from claiming "EXEMPT" status. *Black's Law Dictionary* defines distraint as follows:

> To take as a pledge property of another, and keep it until he performs his obligation.... Also, any detention of personal property, whether lawful or unlawful, for any purpose.

So, the withholding of property (your wages) in payment of taxes that have not yet been assessed and are therefore not owed, if done without your voluntary consent, is done by force—or distraint—and, as such, would be contrary to our professed self-assessment system.

Anyone in the country, therefore, is legally "EXEMPT" from having taxes withheld from his pay the moment he chooses not to assess himself because:

1. No one can be officially assessed by the government *during* the taxable year.

2. No one can be *forced* to assess himself.
3. Taxes cannot legally be withheld by *distraint*.

Therefore, both law and logic dictate that all individuals who no longer wish to assess themselves and have taxes withheld from their pay need to do on a W-4 is to enter "EXEMPT" on line 3.

How the IRS Attempts to Illegally Withhold Taxes by Distraint

The government, however, in order to contravene our self-assessment system and collect taxes by distraint, has placed two immaterial questions on the W-4 Form. They illegally insist that these questions must be answered in the affirmative before an employee can exercise his lawful right not to assess himself. The two questions (3a and 3b) are totally irrelevant to whether or not the government is legally entitled to any portion of your current wages. What relevance, for example, does your 1981 tax status have as to whether or not you have a tax liability for wages received during a given week in 1982? Is the fact that you owed and paid property taxes last year relevant to whether you owe property taxes this year? The point is, what you did or did not "owe," or have a "right to" last year is totally irrelevant to whether you "owe" taxes on weekly wages received *this year*.

Isn't it obvious that these two questions were put on the W-4 Form so that the government could force employees to pay taxes that they don't legally owe? Employees shouldn't let the government get away with it!

If you didn't owe federal income taxes last year and don't intend to assess yourself this year, then you can obviously answer both questions in the affirmative and claim "EXEMPT." Your employer will then no longer be authorized to withhold taxes from your pay. (He will continue to withhold Social Security, though.)

However if you filed a tax return last year and voluntarily assessed a tax against yourself this could interfere with your ability to answer question 3a in the affirmative—*unless* fraud was involved.

Fraud and the W-4 Form

Fraud is defined in *Black's Law Dictionary* as follows:

> An intentional perversion of truth for the purpose of inducing another in reliance upon it to part with some valuable thing belonging to him or to surrender a legal right; a false representation of a matter of fact, whether by words or by conduct, by false or misleading allegations, or by concealment of that which should have been disclosed, which deceives and is intended to deceive another so that he shall act upon it to his legal injury.

What could be a better description of the actions of the IRS?! The IRS Privacy Act Notice was supposed to tell you, *by law*, that the filing of a tax return is *voluntary*. Instead, they led you to believe that you *must* file a tax return and that, in addition, you could be subject to *penalties* if you didn't file. Thus the IRS not only *intentionally*, but *unlawfully* misrepresented "a material fact" in order to induce you "to part with some valuable thing" (the money you paid in taxes) and to "surrender a legal right" (your Fifth Amendment right.) So, anything you filed with the IRS or paid to the IRS as a result of your reliance on their misrepresentations was based on fraud! Of course, if you *knew* that filing was totally voluntary (and you could not be punished in any way for not filing), and if you *knew* that you didn't have to pay any taxes to the IRS or have any money withheld from your wages *until you received a bill from the Secretary of the Treasury,* then what you filed or paid was not based on fraud.

The Consequences of Fraud

According to the United States Supreme Court the consequences of fraud are as follows:

Fraud destroys the validity of everything into which it enters.[1]

Fraud vitiates everything.[2]

Fraud vitiates the most solemn contracts, documents and even judgements.[3]

Since all of your past transactions with the IRS, prior to your reading this book, were undoubtedly based not only on the fraud committed by the IRS, but on their actual violation of the law with respect to what they were *required* to tell you, I suggest that all of these past transactions are *void* and have no validity. Therefore, any current representations you make with respect to these transactions can not have any legal substance.

The Bottom Line

By law, only *you*, and no one else, can determine your withholding status as provided in Section 3402 (n) of the Internal Revenue Code. (See Fig. 5-2)

1. *Nudd* v. *Burrows*
2. *Boyce* v. *Grundy*
3. *U.S.* v. *Throckmorton*

(n) Employees incurring no income tax liability.—Notwithstanding any other provision of this section, an employer shall not be required to deduct and withhold any tax under this chapter upon a payment of wages to an employee if there is in effect with respect to such payment a withholding exemption certificate (in such form and containing such other information as the Secretary may prescribe) furnished to the employer by the employee certifying that the employee—

(1) incurred no liability for income tax imposed under subtitle A for his preceding taxable year, and

(2) anticipates that he will incur no liability for income tax imposed under subtitle A for his current taxable year.

The Secretary shall by regulations provide for the coordination of the provisions of this subsection with the provisions of subsection (f).

Figure 5–2
Internal Revenue Code Section 3402(n)

Note that the law specifically provides that your employer is not "required" to deduct any taxes from your pay if you submit a W-4 certifying that you are "EXEMPT." In addition, a United States District Court has ruled with respect to your W-4:

The employer is not authorized to alter the [W-4] form or dishonor the employee's claim.[4]

So, if you submit an "EXEMPT" W-4 to your employer, he is neither "required" nor "authorized" by law, to withhold any money from your wages in payment of taxes you don't owe.

If taxes are currently being withheld from your pay, all you have to do to stop this withholding is to ask your employer to give you a new W-4 and complete it to

4. *United States* v. *Malinowski*

establish your "EXEMPT" status. By claiming "EX-
EMPT," you will have stopped the withholding and
will have resigned your position as an unpaid tax
assessor!

Workers Can Not Be Forced to File Returns Simply to Get Refunds

The government cannot compel employees to have
taxes withheld from their pay before a correct tax liability is determined, because, if more taxes are withheld
than are ultimately due, an employee is *forced* to file a
tax return simply to get a refund. Thus he is compelled
to give up a constitutional right in order to get his
money back!

I posed the following question to the IRS. "Suppose
that last year I did pay taxes and was not entitled to a
'full refund,' but this year I expect to earn only a few
thousand dollars, and would thus not owe any taxes—
why can't I claim 'EXEMPT'?" I was told that even
under those conditions I would need to have taxes
withheld but that I could file for a refund "next year."
The IRS wanted me to believe that (1) I was required to
pay taxes that even the IRS admitted would not be
owed, and (2) I would be required to surrender a constitutional right in order to get my money back. Such
contentions by the IRS were, of course, preposterous.

Illegal IRS W-4 Harassment

Since the number of employees using the W-4 to
stop the withholding of taxes from their pay has risen
dramatically during the past two years, the IRS (now in
near-panic) is feverishly trying to prevent its legal use.

To do this, it now *illegally* interferes with the legal rights of workers who no longer desire to assess themselves and have taxes taken from their pay. In essence, the IRS is now intruding between employee and employer with respect to an employee's claimed tax status, and, in these cases, they are changing our self-assessment tax system to one of *compulsory payment of taxes before assessment.*

To effect this change, however, the IRS had to figure out a way to intimidate employers, so in 1980 the IRS adopted a new program. Employers were "directed" to send employee W-4 Forms to the IRS whenever employees claimed "EXEMPT" and their wages exceeded $200 per week. In due course, the employers would get a letter from the IRS telling them to disregard the employee's *sworn* W-4 statement and ordering them to withhold taxes on the basis of one withholding allowance, if the employee had claimed an "EXEMPT" status. Can you believe it?!

Such action on the part of the IRS is illegal. As a matter of fact, the IRS *Manual Supplement* of July 31, 1978, in discussing how IRS agents should handle "EXEMPT" W-4's, states:

> The employer has *no legal obligation to intervene with the employee.* However, the Service has found that in many situations, this is the more effective means of correcting an erroneous withholding certificate with the least *inconvenience* to all parties.(emphasis added)

This is proof that even though the IRS knows that employers have no right to interfere with their employees' W-4 Forms, they are, nevertheless, putting *illegal* pressure on employers to do just that!

So, even though there is no law requiring employers to furnish employee W-4 Forms to the IRS or to change an employee's withholding status when "ordered" to do so by the IRS, the IRS gets away with it by relying on bluff, intimidation, and the public's ignorance. Indeed, an Associated Press story from Boston, dated October 31, 1980, quotes Mr. Herbert Mosher, the IRS District Director for Massachusetts, as stating that the "IRS could not enforce a penalty on employers who refused to cooperate with this policy." "But," continued Mosher, "let's face it, no employer wants to incur the wrath of the IRS." So the IRS policy is admittedly based on the intimidation of employers.

Employers should feel free to disregard any such IRS notices and, as Mosher stated, no penalties will result. The law on this is quite clear. An employee has the sole right to determine his withholding status and to claim "EXEMPT." As a matter of fact, employers who do not honor such employee statements do so at their own financial peril, since they could be subject to civil law suits brought against them by their employees in accordance with the principle clearly stated in *United States* v. *Malinowski.*

In any case, the action of the IRS agents, in sending letters to employers telling them to disregard their own employee's sworn statements as to their withholding status, is totally illegal. It is a blatant denial of the due process clause of the United States Constitution and amounts to the deprivaton of a worker's property without a hearing. If an employee presents his employer with a *sworn statement* as to his withholding status, that sworn statement cannot be disregarded just because some yo-yo at the IRS thinks otherwise. If the IRS really believes that an employee's statement is false, then the IRS can recommend to the Justice Department that it bring criminal charges against him for filing a false and fraudulent W-4 Form, as provided in Section 7205 of the Internal Revenue Code. The employee's sworn statement cannot, however, be summarily dismissed *without a formal hearing*.

What the IRS is obviously trying to do in these instances is simply to take advantage of the typical employer's fear of an IRS audit as a basis for intimidating him into not honoring his employees' valid W-4 statements. Such intimidation, however, is against the law and is a violation of Sections 241 and 242 of the United States Criminal Code.

Your Weapons Against the IRS

Sections 241 and 242 of the U. S. Criminal Code (Fig. 5-3) provide you with a stick that you can use against both IRS agents and those employers who attempt to withhold taxes by distraint.

Section 241 makes it a crime for "two or more persons to conspire to injure, oppress, theaten, or intimidate" citizens who attempt to exercise or enjoy a right secured to them by the United States Constitution or the laws of the United States. The laws of the United States provide that workers have the right to determine their own withholding status. If IRS employees conspire with your employer to deny you that right and withhold taxes by distraint, they have broken the law and can be subject to fines, imprisonment, or both. You could not only press criminal charges against them, but you could file a civil lawsuit against them for money damages.

Section 242 makes it a crime for any government employee, acting alone or with others, to attempt to deprive you of any rights or privileges secured to you by the Constitution or the laws of the United States. Any IRS employee who attempts to use his official position to interfere with your right to determine your own withholding status is in open violation of one, and possibly two, criminal statutes.

Sections 241 and 242 can also be effectively used against IRS agents if they seek to threaten or intimidate you at other times. Simply be aware of your rights and when IRS agents attempt to threaten or intimidate you, stand on your rights. If need be, file criminal charges against them for breaking the law (you can swear out such complaints at the office of the U.S.

---

§ 241.   Conspiracy against rights of citizens

If two or more persons conspire to injure, oppress, threaten, or intimidate any citizen in the free exercise or enjoyment of any right or privilege secured to him by the Constitution or laws of the United States, or because of his having so exercised the same; or

If two or more persons go in disguise on the highway, or on the premises of another, with intent to prevent or hinder his free exercise or enjoyment of any right or privilege so secured—

They shall be fined not more than $10,000 or imprisoned not more than ten years, or both; and if death results, they shall be subject to imprisonment for any term of years or for life.

§ 242.   Deprivation of rights under color of law

Whoever, under color of any law, statute, ordinance, regulation, or custom, willfully subjects any inhabitant of any State, Territory, or District to the deprivation of any rights, privileges, or immunities secured or protected by the Constitution or laws of the United States, or to different punishments, pains, or penalties, on account of such inhabitant being an alien, or by reason of his color, or race, than are prescribed for the punishment of citizens, shall be fined not more than $1,000 or imprisoned not more than one year, or both; and if death results shall be subject to imprisonment for any term of years or for life.

Figure 5-3   Your Stick Against The IRS
Sections 241 and 242 of the United States Criminal Code

attorney), and, in addition, you can sue them civilly for financial damages.[5]

Of course, you should have proof of such threats and intimidations through the testimony of witnesses, by having it on tape, or by having other documented proof. Any correspondence sent by the IRS to your employer stating that he is not to comply with your own sworn declaration as to your withholding status is clear documentation of a violation of Section 242 on the part of any IRS official who signs such a letter.

In summary, there is no law that requires employees to have federal income taxes withheld from their pay without their *total* consent. This does not mean, however, that all employees will be able to immediately stop such illegal garnishments of taxes from their wages without a hassle. Those employees who work for employers who can be intimidated by the IRS might encounter some temporary resistance, but the material in this book should enable any employee to overcome that problem.

Illegal W-4 Prosecutions

Through this chapter we have shown that Americans have a legal right to use W-4's to prevent the withholding of taxes. However, in order to intimidate Americans from exercising this right, the courts have occasionally prosecuted Americans who claimed "EXEMPT" to prevent the deduction of taxes from their pay. While relatively few of these prosecutions have taken place, it still might be helpful to know just how such prosecutions can be prevented.

5. See *Bivens v. Six Unknown Federal Narcotics Agents*

First of all, in order to be found guilty of filing a false and fraudulent W-4, the W-4 Form must be introduced at trial and used against the person charged. However, unlike a tax return that is filed voluntarily, a W-4 is compelled. It is compelled because, if an individual does not file a W-4, his employer is required by law to deduct taxes as if he were a single person who did not claim *any* allowances, according to Section 3402(l) and Section 3401 (e) of the Internal Revenue Code.

So individuals who do *not* file W-4 Forms are *punished* by having the maximum amount of taxes taken from their pay. To prevent this type of financial punishment and to prevent what would amount to an illegal garnishing of their wages by the government and the taking of taxes *by distraint*, workers are *forced* to complete a W-4. Therefore, completing a W-4 is actually *compelled*, and it cannot be introduced and used against an individual in a criminal trial. Since W-4's themselves cannot be introduced (if proper objections are raised and argued) no one can lawfully be convicted for the "crime" of allegedly filing a false one!

This issue has never, to my knowledge, been raised at any trial involving the alleged filing of a false W-4. In my view, if this issue had been raised, all such charges would have to have been dropped. So, an understanding of this issue by the public should also eliminate any potential government threat to charge anybody with filing a false or fraudulent W-4. Of course, no one could file a false W-4 based upon his understanding of the material in this book, but given the past conduct of federal courts in these matters, it's nice to know that you have this additional protection.

6

No One Need Submit to an IRS Audit

Only the rare taxpayer would be likely to know that he could refuse to produce his records to IRS agents.

United States Court of Appeals
United States v. *Dickerson* (1969)

What the public fears most from the IRS is a tax audit. This can strike terror into the heart of the most redoubtable citizen. Such audits can involve, of course, substantial legal and accounting fees, while diverting precious time from the running of a business. I have known businessmen who have had weeks of valuable time consumed by IRS audits. What is ironic about all of this, is that audits are unnecessary, and no citizen is legally required to submit to them.

I stopped paying federal income taxes in 1974, and since then, neither my corporation nor I has ever undergone an IRS audit, despite numerous IRS efforts to get me to do so—even including the IRS sending my corporation a summons to produce its books and records. But in all of these years, neither my corporation nor I has turned over one scrap of paper to the IRS. Let me share an article, written by reporter Ken Cruickshank, who was present at one audit attempt. (This first appeared in the June 26, 1976, edition of the *Hartford Courant*.)

Writer Taxes IRS

by Ken Cruickshank

Shades of Vivien Kellems! A catered tax audit.

Well. sort of catered. There were bagles, rolls, juice and coffee for the troops (reporters and anyone who happened to be interested) and for the IRS auditor. too,· if he wanted them (it turned out he didn't).

The scene was the apartment of Irwin A. Schiff in Hamden. Schiff, author of the book "The Biggest Con: How the Government is Fleecing You" and numerous articles on tax inequities, had, it seems, received a letter from the Internal Revenue Service about his 1974 and 1975 tax returns.

Small wonder. Each return ran to about 100 pages and gave the IRS every reason under the sun why Schiff felt no obligation whatsoever to pay his taxes. What the returns didn't give were any figures pertaining to Schiff's income or assets.

So Schiff got this letter telling him an IRS auditor would meet with him at his home on May 26. "Please have your income. expense and deduction records available." the letter said.

Instead of flying into an instant panic. as most of us would do, Schiff calmly told the IRS that the date set was inconvenient and, finally, after some haggling, agreed to meet a Joseph F. O'Brien. Internal Revenue agent, at his (Schiff's) home at 10 a.m. Thursday.

O'Brien believed he was coming for a simple audit. Schiff decided it was to be a public event.

"I don't have to give him my records." Schiff said to a mixed bag of reporters and interested parties who had turned up for the pre-audit pep talk a half hour before the IRS agent was due. "But most people would be intimidated and give the IRS every record they wanted. Then the IRS could prosecute on the basis of that informatoin. That's self-incrimination!"

Schiff claimed the whole business of IRS audits is "a fraud and intimidation."

"The IRS agent has no more judicial standing than my postman." he said, "yet they scare the heck out of people."

If you get the idea Schiff does not like the tax system in the United States, you would be right. In fact he claims the government, with the gullible compliance of the U.S. public, is actively fleecing its citizens and violating several of its own laws in doing so.

The standard income tax form 1040 he calls "a confession." He especially objects to the phrase which says you have answered the questions to the best of your knowledge and ability "under penalty of perjury" and urges people to cross out that line when they send in their forms — if they send in any at all.

"It's pure self-incrimination if you sign it." he said. "Once you have signed

IRWIN A. SCHIFF

that line you leave yourself open to all kinds of penalties — but they never warn you about that."

At 10 a.m. sharp there was a knock at the door.

Enter IRS agent O'Brien, obviously shocked by the array of seats and the hasty scribbling in notebooks as he entered.

He sat down and Schiff asked him if he could make a tape recording of the audit.

As Schiff predicted. O'Brien said he had been instructed by his superior to leave immediately if any tape recording was insisted upon. After clarifying that point. Schiff shuts off his tape recorder.

"The government doesn't want a clear record of their intimidation tactics." Schiff said later. "They never let you record them."

After warning O'Brien that he, in Schiff's opinion, was leaving himself liable to criminal prosecution under an obscure civil rights statute. Schiff refused to show his records to the IRS agent after O'Brien admitted the records could be used against Schiff in court.

More haranguing by Schiff ended in a standoff. O'Brien was offered a bagle. He turned it down.

"I think you're auditing me." he joked during the procedure and, afterwards, said laughingly:

"You really put me through the wringer." before he left.

The audit — or nonaudit — was over. The IRS now knows the battle lines are drawn and so does Schiff, who didn't seem perturbed.

Schiff thinks he has a good case against the government and feels the IRS will have a tough time prosecuting.

"They may not dare," says an observer. "If he won on constitutional grounds, it would ruin the whole tax system."

So Schiff wins round 1.

But O'Brien, before he left, had uttered some prophetic words.

"We'll be back." he said.

Nonpayer's IRS Interview Taxing for Agents

By MARK MELADY

NORTH HAVEN — Irwin A. Schiff, who passionately refuses to pay income tax because he claims his only source of income is federal promissory notes — more widely known as dollarbills — was summoned by the IRS Thursday for an examination of some tax records.

He showed up to answer the summons with four friends, five members of the press, two cardboard boxes marked "tax records and other secret stuff" and a copy of the U.S. Constitution.

The entourage was met by three apprehensive IRS agents and everyone adjourned to a little office, whereupon Schiff cordially said to the agents, "Sit down, make yourself comfortable, I've got some questions to ask."

From the proceedings that followed it was impossible to determine who was the summonor and who was the summonee.

Schiff, a Hamden investment and insurance specialist, has not paid any income tax since 1973. High among his multitude of reasons for skipping the annual mandatory event, is his insistence that he hasn't earned any money.

Federal reserve notes, commonly accepted as U.S. currency, are defined by Schiff as "accounts receivable."

Besides that, Schiff contends, paying income tax would implicate him in treasonous taxing and monetary policies that subvert our republican form of government and will lead to rioting, pillaging and bloodshed.

Rioting and pillaging aside, what the three IRS agents really wanted to see Thursday was a few records.

In May the IRS tried to go over Schiff's personal income through a conventional audit. When agent John F. O'Brien showed up at Schiff's home, however, he found reporters sitting around munching bagels and Schiff smiling over a tape recorder.

The audit attempt ended when Schiff asked O'Brien if anything he said during the audit could be used against him in court. O'Brien said it could. Schiff said that would violate his fifth amendment rights. O'Brien said he would be back.

But instead the IRS turned its keen attention to the corporation of which Schiff is president, Irwin A. Schiff Inc.

O'Brien began writing letters addressing Schiff as "Gentlemen" and attempting to arrange a convenient time to conduct an audit of Schiff Inc.

Schiff, the person, responded with "Dear John" letters telling O'Brien to be mindful of his dress because TV people would probably be present. He refused to meet in "the murky bowels" of the IRS.

The inability of both parties to agree on a time and place led to the IRS summons demanding Schiff be at the IRS office, murky or not, at 10 a.m. Thursday.

So there was Schiff, with a handkerchief in his breast pocket and the Constitution in his hand, lecturing police O'Brien, who had dutifully sat down, about the law. The law, said Schiff, gives a taxpayer the right to investigate why the IRS has issued him a summons.

The law, according to Schiff, also prohibits the IRS from compelling a taxpayer to turn over records of a corporation in which he is a shareholder if the real intent is to audit the shareholder's personal income.

O'Brien told Schiff that one of the reasons the IRS was examining the record of Schiff Inc. was to review Schiff's personal income. Schiff felt compelled to read the agents the law concerning conspiracy to deprive someone of his Constitutional rights.

To enhance his investigation, Schiff said he had developed a public servant questionnaire, which he produced.

Schiff's first question to O'Brien was where he lived.

"You don't have to answer that," counseled agent Frank Trager, a grade school chum of Schiff's.

"I don't want to answer these questions," said O'Brien.

"You want to plead the Fifth then," said Schiff as he wrote on the questionnaire, "Fifth Amendment plea."

Meanwhile IRS Group Manager Peter Abbagnaro had excused himself from the room to see if he could find an IRS regulation that could reduce the number of people in the room, namely Schiff's four friends and the five members of the press.

He found one after a while and reported back to the gathering that the IRS had the right to set the time, place and conditions for an examination.

The negotiations over the conditions of the meeting turned out to be moot, however, because Schiff claimed he needed to question a supervisory agent who was not present to complete his investigation.

When the IRS failed to get my personal records, they switched their efforts to my corportion. They failed in that attempt, too, as the *Hartford Courant* reported on December 17, 1976, under the caption "Nonpayer's Interview Taxing for Agents" shown on (page 79).

The IRS Audit—A Part of Voluntary Compliance

The reason you cannot be required to submit to an IRS audit, is that an audit is also a part of "voluntary compliance." As you already know, the government cannot use compelled testimony against you, so if the government requires you to turn over your books and records to the IRS, it cannot use any of that information against you in matters relating to income tax evasion, the levying of additional fines and penalties, or criminal offenses unrelated to taxes. Thus, the very purpose of the IRS audit would vanish. The IRS conducts audits to secure information that the government can use against taxpayers, if necessary. To do that, the material must be obtained *voluntarily,* and if citizens do not volunteer, they cannot be audited!

The following excerpt from Section 342.12 of the IRS's own *Handbook for Special Agents*[2] admits this:

1. This article reflects my earlier belief that citzens had no tax liability because they were only paid in nonredeemable (and thus, intrinsically worthless) notes issued by the Federal Reserve, a private banking syndicate. While this view is correct, I subsequently discovered that there are other, more fundamental reasons why citizens have no tax liability, and so I stopped using the "money argument."

2. Copies of this handbook can be obtained by sending ⌀5.00 to Freedom of Information Room, Internal Revenue Service, 1111 Constitution Avenue, N.W., Washington, D.C. 20224.

An individual may *refuse* to exhibit his books and records for examination on the ground that compelling him to do so might violate his right against self-incrimination under the Fifth Amendment and constitute an illegal search and seizure under the Fourth Amendment.[3] *(emphasis added)*

So, here is your official proof that you need not submit to an IRS audit. If you do, you are waiving your Fourth and Fifth Amendment rights!

Section 342.15 of the aforementioned IRS handbook, entitled "Waiver of Constitutional Rights," provides additional material on the same theme, as seen below.

(1) The privilege against self-incrimination must be specifically claimed or it will be considered to have been waived. In the Nicola case (note 17) the taxpayer permitted a revenue agent to examine his books and records. The taxpayer was indicted for income tax evasion and invoked his constitutional rights under the Fifth Amendment for the first time at the trial, by objecting to the revenue agent's testimony concerning his findings. The court said, on the question of waiver :

"But he did not refuse to supply the information required. Did he waive his privilege? The constitutional guarantee is for the benefit of the witness and unless invoked is deemed to be waived. Vajtauer v. Commissioner of Immigration (supra). Was it necessary for the defendant to invoke it in the first place before the revenue agent or could he wait until his trial on indictment for attempting to evade a part of his income tax? (Cases cited) * * * *it was necessary for him to claim immunity before the Government agent and refuse to produce his books.* After the Government had gotten possession of the information with his consent, it was too late for him then to claim constitutional immunity."

---

3. Actually the handbook misstates the reason. The issue is one of being "a witness" against oneself, not one of "self-incrimination."

Nicola was indicted for income tax evasion and "objected for the first time" *at his trial* to an IRS agent's testimony, which included information given to him by Nicola at an audit. Note, however, the position taken by the court concerning Nicola's attempt to use the Fifth Amendment as a defense at his trial. The court denied Nicola's objection on the ground that Nicola should have raised the question of the Fifth Amendment at his audit and *refused* at that time to turn over his books. However, once he gave his books to the IRS, it was too late to prevent the information from being used against him. I can imagine the following colloquy taking place at Nicola's trial:

Judge: Look! You voluntarily gave the agent your books. You can't come in here *now* and take the Fifth. You should have done that at your audit and refused to give the IRS agent your books.
Nicola: But, Your Honor, nobody told me that my Fifth Amendment right protected me in that setting. I thought that I was required to give my books to the IRS.
Judge: No, dummy, you didn't have to give them a thing.
Nicola: Gee Judge, where were you when I needed you?

The Fourth Amendment to the United States Constitution

The Fourth Amendment to the Constitution states:

The right of the people to be secure in their person, houses, *papers* and effects against unreasonable searches and seizures shall not be violated. (emphasis added)

A reasonable search is one where the government has probable cause to believe that one possesses something illegal, such as untaxed liquor or cigarettes, gambling paraphernalia, marked money, or perhaps a murder weapon. A search warrant signed by a judge and based on probable cause, allows law enforcement personnel to search one's premises for the specific item which, if found, might indicate that a crime has been committed.

But an IRS search through your books and records is a "fishing expedition," pure and simple. That is, the government doesn't have any probable cause to believe that you did something wrong or that you have sworn falsely on your return. The IRS merely wants to fish through your records to see whether you *may* have done something wrong. Such "fishing expeditions" are barred by the Constitution. Thus, the only way the government can get your books and records is if you give them up voluntarily.

This principle was clearly upheld in the definitive Supreme Court ruling in the case of *Boyd* vs *The United States*:

> It does not require actual entry upon premises and search for and seizure of papers to constitute an unreasonable search and seizure within the meaning of the Fourth Amendment; a compulsory production of a party's private books and papers, to be used against himself or his property in a criminal or penal proceeding, or for a forfeiture, is within the spirit or meaning of the Amendment.

Thus, the Supreme Court ruled that your Fourth and Fifth Amendment rights provide ample grounds for

keeping your financial records out of the hands of the
IRS.

Americans Get Tricked into Being Audited

Since taxpayers are not required to submit to IRS
audits, the IRS has to trick them into it. The letter that I
received from the IRS in May of 1976 (Fig. 6-1), is typical
of the type of letter that the IRS uses for this purpose.

Observe how cleverly the letter is worded. The agent
very innocently tells me that he wants to meet with me to
"discuss [my] tax liability for the years 1974 and 1975."
There is nothing in his letter that states that the meeting
is for the purpose of auditing or examining my books and
records or that I am required to turn them over. The letter
does request, however, that I "please" have my books
and records "available." From such language, taxpayers
assume that the agents are legally entitled to see their
books and records. This, of course, is exactly the false
impression that the IRS hopes to convey. Most taxpayers
do not notice (when receiving similar letters) that, while
the letter asks that books and records be "available,"
there is nothing that states that they are to be made
"available" *to the IRS agent!* In his letter, the agent
further states, "I will be at your residence ... on Wednesday, May 26, 1976, at 9:00 A.M." The agent does not even
bother to ask me if the time is convenient, so the letter
carries the implication that I am being ordered to be there
at that time. This is typical of the style used by IRS
agents who, because taxpayers are not required to meet
with them, use intimidating language to get them to do
so.

In my Untax Seminars that I have conducted all
over America since 1977, and in my *Freedom Kit*, I ex-

Address any reply to:

Department of the Treasury

110 Washington Avenue, 3rd Floor
North Haven, CT 06473

District Director

Internal Revenue Service

Date: In reply refer to:

May 19, 1976

▷   Mr. Irwin A. Schiff
2405 Whitney Avenue
Hamden, CT 06518

Dear Mr. Schiff:

I would like to make an appointment with you to discuss your
tax liability for the years 1974 and 1975. I will be at your
residence, 2405 Whitney Avenue, Apt. 506, Hamden, Connecticut,
on Wednesday, May 26, 1976, at 9:00 A.M. Please have your
income, expense and deduction records available.

If the above appointment date is not feasible with you, please
call me at 432-2085 in order to arrange a mutual date for the
appointment. My office address is 110 Washington Avenue, 3rd
Floor, North Haven, Connecticut, 06473.

Please note Publication 876 is enclosed.

Very truly yours,

John F. O'Brien
Internal Revenue Agent

Figure 6-1

plain how citizens can deal with this type of IRS intimidation and perhaps employ a little reverse intimidation
of their own. One procedure, for example, is to telephone
the IRS agent on the day before the scheduled audit
(preferably late-afternoon) and simply break the appointment. Any number of good excuses should suggest
themselves. That thousands of Americans are, indeed,
adopting this policy became clear on June 10, 1981, when
Roscoe L. Egger, the current IRS Commissioner, stated
at a congressional hearing on the problems that the IRS
was having with the growing national tax rebellion:

> ... Processing tax protester cases is much more difficult
> than other cases ... Tax protesters often have strongly
> resisted our efforts to obtain information through frequent
> cancellation and rescheduling of interview appointments;
> failure to keep scheduled appointments; demanding that all
> questions or communications be made in writing; and with-
> holding of records that were specifically identified and re-
> quested by the examiners, thus necessitating the issuance
> and court enforcement of summonses to obtain any tax-
> payer and third party records.

So the Commissioner of the IRS is upset because more
and more Americans are refusing to surrender their constitutional rights or to be intimidated by the IRS!

Asking IRS agents to "put in writing" questions
that they want to "discuss," was another tactic that I
have long advocated. Mr Egger confirmed that these
techniques are, indeed, being employed by growing
numbers of Americans who no longer tremble when they
hear from the IRS, but can now give the IRS a dose of its
own medicine.

In any case, I made and broke several appointments
with the agent before meeting with him. I finally had the
meeting simply to demonstrate to fellow citizens that the
IRS does not have the power to force an individual to
reveal his books and records.

The Two Magical Questions

It was during this long-awaited meeting that IRS
agent O'Brien extended his hand across the table at
which we were both sitting, and said, "May I please see
your books and records?" Had I voluntarily handed

them over to him, I would *at that moment* have waived my Fourth and Fifth Amendment rights. Instead, I replied, "Mr. O'Brien, your letter merely requests that my books be available. They are *available* here, where I can refer to them, if needed." O'Brien, however, insisted that he was there to see my books and records; so I asked, "But, Mr. O'Brien, where does your letter state that my books and records are to be made available to *you?*" He again insisted that his letter provided for the auditing of my books and records. It didn't, of course, but the letter that served as the model for O'Brien's letter was obviously designed to allow IRS agents to gain by stealth what they couldn't gain by legal compulsion—access to a taxpayer's books and records.

It was then that I sprang on O'Brien my Two Magical Questions, which will stop any IRS audit dead in its tracks. "Mr. O'Brien," I said, "if I turn my books and records over to you, can the government use any of the information against me?" (Since there were witnesses present, I could confidently expect a truthful answer.) "Well, yes," he replied. Then I asked, "Do I have a legal obligation to give you any information that can be used against me?" He then very reluctantly said, "No." At that moment, he realized that he had told me that I didn't have to give him my books and records, so he immediately stood up and prepared to leave, so I said, "But, Mr. O'Brien, your letter said you wanted to *discuss* my tax liability for the years 1974 and 1975. I am fully prepared to do that." O'Brien did not really want to "discuss" my tax liablility, as stated in his letter; he wanted to examine my books and records, which was not stated in his letter. Since I couldn't be tricked into turning over my books and records, he decided to leave, as there was now no point to the interview.

Audit Letters From IRS Agents Shouldn't Frighten You

When citizens receive letters similar to the one I received, they do not have to take any notice of them, since such letters do not have the force of law—which is why they must try to sound intimidating. (You can give such letters about as much weight as you would give one addressed to "Present Occupant.") If, after receiving such a letter, you decide you do not want to be audited, you can do any one of the following:

1. Write a letter to the IRS agent asking him to put any questions he has into writing.
2. Call or write the agent and inform him that, since you do not wish to waive your Fourth and Fifth Amendment rights, you must decline his offer to audit you.
3. Keep the appointment, claim your constitutional rights, and refuse to turn over your books and records at that time.

The Powerless IRS Summons

If the IRS really wants to see your books and records, they might risk sending you an IRS summons, which *does* have some legal muscle behind it. While individuals are free to disregard *routine* letters from the IRS *requesting audits,*[5] an IRS summons has the force of law. If you receive one and don't appear, criminal penal-

---

5. I don't, however, recommend that *any* letter from the IRS be totally disregarded (especially those concerning possible assessments), but it was never the purpose of this book to deal with all IRS communications.

ties can apply. If you ever receive an IRS summons and do not wish to be audited, just show up with your books and records (sealed in cardboard boxes) and ask the Two Magical Questions. You'll get the same answers, after which you can gather up your books and records and leave. Thus, you will have complied with the summons, but the IRS will still not have gained access to your private books and records. However, the likelihood of your getting an IRS summons is slim, as Section 363, of the IRS's *Handbook for Special Agents*, makes clear:

> When a taxpayer or a witness refuses to submit requested information, all surrounding circumstances should be fully considered before a summons is issued. The likely importance of the desired information should be carefully weighed against the time and expense of obtaining it, the probability of having to institute court action, *and the adverse effect on voluntary compliance by others if the enforcement efforts are not successful.* (emphasis added)

In addition, Section 6 of the *IRS Supplement* of January 10, 1979, states:

> However, summons of a taxpayer's books and records for return information is *not recommended*.

The above excerpts from the Internal Revenue manuals show that the IRS does not like to use summonses, since "enforcement efforts" might prove unsuccessful and, thus, adversely affect "voluntary compliance *by others*." In other words, the IRS realizes that, if a taxpayer demonstrates that he doesn't have to turn over his personal records, even though he receives *an official summons*, it would be a powerful demonstration to others that no one is required, in any circumstances, to turn over his own books and records. This, of course, is information that the IRS would desperately like to keep from the public. That is why the IRS Supplement states that the use of an IRS summons "is not recommended."

The ability to use one's Fifth Amendment right to defeat an IRS summons is also contained in Section 342.12 of the *Handbook for Special Agents*.

> The privilege against self-incrimination does not permit a taxpayer to refuse to obey a summons issued under IRC 7602 or a court order directing his appearance. He is required to appear and cannot use the Fifth Amendment as an excuse for failure to do so, although he may exercise it in connection with specific questions. He cannot refuse to bring his records, *but may decline to submit them for inspection on Constitutional grounds*. (emphasis added)[6]

While the IRS's own handbook states that individuals must obey a summons by making a physical appearance, it also confirms that they can, on constitutional grounds, still refuse to submit their books and records for inspection.

It should also be obvious that if individuals can, on constitutional grounds, refuse to produce their books and records for inspection, they can also, on the same grounds, refuse to submit tax returns, since the information provided on a tax return can be used against individuals to the same extent as information found in an individual's books and records! Thus, if an individual doesn't have to submit the one, on constitutional grounds, simple logic indicates that he doesn't have to submit the other, either.

I could not use my Two Magical Questions at my

6. Again the handbook incorrectly raises the question of "self-incrimination".

summons proceedings, since the records summoned did not belong to me, but to my corporation, and the Fifth Amendment only applies to individual citizens, not to corporations.

This being the case, I had to find another basis for keeping those records from the IRS. I did a little research and discovered that "a Corporation is not bound to produce its books to the assessor on an inquiry into the income of its shareholders."[7] In addition, I discovered that when a summons is issued, "the taxpayer is entitled to investigate, by way of discovery, the Internal Revenue Service's purpose, where such purpose has been put in issue and may affect the legality of the summons."[8] I also found that individuals may "challenge the summons on any appropriate grounds."[9] So, armed with these cases and using a public servant's questionnaire[10] to help me conduct my "investigation", I was able to frustrate the IRS's attempt to get my corporation's books and records, as described in the *Hartford Courant's* article of December 17, 1976. And they haven't attempted to audit me or my corporation since!

An IRS Audit Punishes the Cooperative Citizen

If you really stop and think about the rationale behind an IRS audit, you must be struck by the utter absurdity of it all. The government, it must be remem-

---

7. Chadwick (DC Mass)
8. *United States* v. *Roundtree*
9. *U.S.* v. *Powell,* and *Reisman* v. *Caplan*
10. A questionnaire created by those in the tax-patriot movement to elicit information from government employees who were trying to get information from us. Questions reflected information that we had a right to know under the Privacy Act and related laws.

bered, is legally responsible to determine each taxpayer's liability *without any help from the taxpayer*. This, admittedly is a big job and probably couldn't be accomplished at all if John Q. Citizen did not trustingly volunteer to pitch in and help. Often at great expense and inconvenience to himself, John Q. figures out his own taxes and then, like a good little boy, sends in his check—after swearing under penalty of perjury that he computed it correctly. And what does he get for all his trouble? Well, an obviously ungrateful and inconsiderate government has the nerve to tell John Q. Citizen that it doesn't believe his sworn statement and therefore, insists on putting him through the wringer of an IRS tax audit. In the process, John Q. runs the risks of additional fines and penalties, or even of being charged with income tax evasion.[11] This is what helpful John Q. Citizen often gets for voluntarily helping the government to assess his taxes.

As a United States Court of Appeals observed in U.S. v. Dickerson,[12]

> Who would believe the ironic truth that the cooperative taxpayer fares much worse than the individual who relies upon his constitutional rights!

To suggest, therefore, that helpful citizens should even be subject to IRS audits is, when you think about it, absurd. If the federal government is not going to accept

11. Income tax evasion is nothing more than being charged with the crime of swearing falsely on a tax return. You cannot be charged with income tax evasion (a felony) unless you file a tax return. So, one of the risks you create when you file a tax return is the possibility that you will be charged with income tax evasion.
12. Quoting from, Paul Lipton, "Constitutional Rights in Criminal Tax Investigation," 45 F. R. D. 323 336 (1968).

your sworn statement as to what you believe your tax liability to be, then why bother giving them one? If the government takes the position that it can make you "prove" sworn statements, voluntarily given, then does it make any sense to provide them with such statements? Why run the risk of your sworn statements being held in error?

In essence, being threatened with an IRS audit is the penalty that cooperative citizens pay for voluntarily filing tax returns. If individuals filed no tax returns, they would never have this problem. The reason is simple. By filing a tax return, the taxpayer swears to having received a certain amount of taxable income, which he then reduces by claimed exemptions and deductions. However, the IRS often takes the position that, once a taxpayer admits to taxable income, all subsequent deductions are granted with the sufferance of the IRS; if the taxpayer can't justify the deductions to some agent's satisfaction, they can be disallowed and a higher tax imposed.

So, while no one is required to be audited, those filing tax returns may have to face the additional inconvenience and expense of an audit in order to justify and protect the deductions shown on their returns. If tax returns are not filed this is never a problem.

Third Party Records

While the IRS cannot get your personal records, they *can* get records about you from third parties, such as accountants (for which reason you may not want your accountant to keep any of your tax records). Also, the IRS can subpoena your bank records and get copies of your cancelled checks, and they can subpoena information from people with whom you do business. While the IRS never succeeded in getting any of my personal or corporate records, they did manage to get copies of my personal and corporate checks by subpoenaing them from the bank.[13] However, they had to pay my bank $2,000 in clerical and microfilming costs. Because U.S. banks do not resist the government's efforts to get your cancelled checks (which contain personal information and which were created by you), which I believe should be protected by your Fourth and Fifth Amendment rights, you can take your own steps to protect your records and your privacy.

For the last four years I have made out my checks using a nonreproducible pen—the type used by artists in making advertising layouts. The special ink usually cannot be picked up by photocopiers and banks' microfilm equipment. So, if you use these pens and the IRS gains access to your bank records, apart from your bank statement, they'll only get blank checks to look at, while you, of course, will still have the legible originals, should you need them. This nonreproducible ink is a peacock blue, and I recommend that it be used on blue-green checks. The pens usually sell for about one dollar in stationery and art stores.[14]

In the final analysis filing a tax return is a little like voluntarily putting your own head into a noose offered by the IRS and trusting them not to hang you. If you don't want to worry about IRS audits—then just stop filing. The choice is yours to make!

---

13. Taxpayers now, however, have a right to intervene to prevent banks from turning over these records. This was not the case when the IRS got my bank records.

14. If you cannot secure these pens locally, you can order them, in lots of five or more, at ¢1.00 per pen, from Freedom Books.

7

How the Public Gets Brainwashed

In a recent conversation with an official at the Internal Revenue Service, I was amazed when he told me that, "If the taxpayers of this country ever discover that the Internal Revenue Service operates on 90% BLUFF, the entire system will collapse."

Senator Henry Bellmon (1969)

The Internal Revenue Service has three functions:

1. Collect taxes.
2. Collect more taxes.
3. Collect even more taxes.

Since our income tax, as you know, is based upon voluntary compliance and self-assessment, the federal government would collect very little if the IRS correctly explained to the American public what this meant. Therefore, the real job of the IRS is to mislead and confuse the public regarding our tax laws so that it can collect revenue for the government. You must be aware of this whenever you speak to IRS agents. Remember, their job is not to explain the law or to help you, but to collect taxes from you; if they have to mislead you to do that, they will.

Your Federal Income Tax

For use in preparing
1980 Returns

Department
of the
Treasury
Internal
Revenue
Service

Publication 17
(Rev. Nov. 80)

A——The explanations and examples in this publication reflect the official <u>interpretation</u> by the Internal Revenue Service of:
- Tax laws enacted by Congress, and
- Treasury regulations, and
- Court decisions.

Disclaimer!

The publication covers some subjects on which certain courts have taken positions more favorable to taxpayers than the official position of the Service. Until these interpretations are resolved by higher court decisions, or otherwise, the publication will continue to present the viewpoint of the Service.

All taxpayers have appeal rights within the Service and may appeal to the courts when they do not agree with positions taken by the Service. Appeal procedures are described in Chapter 6.

Figure 7–1

IRS Publications Don't Explain the Law

All IRS manuals designed for public consumption (including the instructional booklet that accompanies a 1040) are worded to mislead the public regarding (1) its legal obligations under our tax laws, and (2) the real meaning of "income" as it applies to income taxes. For example, please read Fig. 7-1,the notice that appears on the inside front cover of the IRS's *Publication 17*, which is the most comprehensive tax manual that the IRS provides to the public. This unobtrusive, innocent looking statement amounts to an official "disclaimer" concerning the information in that manual, though I am sure that the public doesn't even notice, let alone understand, the significance of this disclaimer.

When the public reads *Publication 17* and similar IRS materials, it generally believes that what it is reading is "tax law," and not merely the IRS's interpretation of that law. But examine what the disclaimer says (Note A):

> The explanations and examples in this publication reflect the official *interpretation* by the Internal Revenue Service of:
>> Tax laws enacted by Congress, and
>> Treasury regulations, and
>> Court decisions.

This disclaimer has discreetly informed us that the tax information contained in the manual is not the law, but merely the IRS's "interpretation" of it, and the IRS will undoubtedly interpret the law in a manner most beneficial to itself and its mission, the collection of taxes. This is even admitted in the next paragraph:

> The publication covers some subjects on which certain *courts have taken positions more favorable to taxpayers than*

the official positon of the Service. Until these interpretations are resolved by higher court decisions, or otherwise, the publication will continue to present the viewpoint of the Service.

Here the IRS unabashedly admits that its publications do not present the law, but only the law as the IRS wants you to understand it. It even admits that its manual will present positions that may actually be contrary to the decisions of United States courts! The higher court referred to in its disclaimer is the Supreme Court, and the IRS openly admits to not being influenced by the decisions of any court lower than the Supreme Court. The truth is, the IRS does not even feel bound by decisions of the Supreme Court, since the Supreme Court has defined the meaning of taxable "income" as something entirely different from what the IRS tells the public. The Supreme Court has ruled that taxable "income," as used in our income tax laws, actually means a "gain" or a "profit." The Supreme Court has ruled that a tax on "income" is, in reality, a tax that can only apply to corporate profits. Futhermore, there is nothing in the Internal Revenue Code that provides for or allows the federal government to levy a direct tax on such things as wages, alimony, dividends, rents, commissions, royalties, and similar items. Such items are simply not subject to a direct tax under our laws. Don't let anybody tell you otherwise.[1]

Now you know that the IRS does not tell you the law, but only its interpretation of it. The IRS, however, manages to keep this distinction secret from the public.

Few Americans ever read the actual law, as contained in the Internal Revenue Code, much less read court decisions that have relevance to that law. Nearly

1. See Irwin Schiff's, *Why No One Can Have Taxable Income,* soon to be released by Freedom Books.

everyone relies entirely on the IRS's biased interpretation of the law. Incidentally, if the IRS does not need to be bound by the U.S. courts' interpretations of our tax laws, why should private citizens be bound by IRS interpretations? By what authority is the IRS's interpretations more binding upon private citizens than the interpretations of our courts are binding on the IRS? Is not the IRS suggesting, therefore, that even judges are not capable of understanding our tax laws?

Can you conceive of the FBI putting out a pamphlet stating that "even though certain courts have taken positions more favorable to citizens than the official position of the FBI, the FBI will continue to make arrests based upon its own interpretation of the law until these interpretations are resolved by the Supreme Court"?

Since the IRS doesn't feel bound by court decisions from the Supreme Court on down, how can citizens figure out their own taxes according to the law? They can't. Besides, IRS agents can't accurately figure out anybody's income taxes, even using their own interpretations. Ralph Nader's Tax Reform Research Group prepared twenty-two identical tax reports, based on a fictional couple with one child, and submitted them to twenty-two IRS offices around the country. Each office that received one calculated a different tax from the same figures! The office in Flushing, New York, for example, determined that the couple was entitled to an $811.96 refund, while the one in Portland, Oregon, found that the couple *owed* the government an additional $52.14.

This illustration, together with the IRS's admission that even federal judges can't figure out the law, must render the entire Internal Revenue Code "void for vagueness." (This is a *fundamental* legal principle known to every freshman law student, which holds that if a law is vague or ambiguous, it is automatically null and void and without effect). If this basic legal principle can be said to have any application at all, then how can the Internal Revenue Code be enforced by any legitimate court?

In any case, since the IRS has demonstrated that (1) it cannot calculate an individual's taxes accurately, and (2) it disregards court decisions when advising taxpayers concerning the law, why should you presume that you can accurately calculate your taxes according to the law? If you let the Secretary of the Treasury figure out your tax, you can't have these problems.

In the final analysis, the IRS is the last agency you would want to use for an interpretation of the tax law as a basis for figuring out your taxes. The reason is simple, as I have already stated: the IRS is not in business to educate you, but to get your money. If they interpret the law for you, you should understand that their interpretation will be designed not to interfere with or diminish their ability to collect taxes (the public is continually fooled on this issue).

The following comparison might help put the IRS's true role into perspective. Let us suppose that a department store hired a collection agency to collect its delinquent accounts. Let us further assume that the collection agency, in contacting one of those accounts, was told that the person did not pay his bill because the merchandise had been received defective and the store had refused to exchange it. The point is that whether these statements are true or false, the collection agency's only purpose is to get the money—which is the only way it makes money. It is not there to advise individuals conscientiously concerning their legal rights with respect to that debt. The IRS functions in precisely the same way; it is merely a *collection agency* for the federal government. So remember, the IRS is in business for only one reason—to get your money. It is not in business to teach you the law or to see to it that the law is honestly or correctly applied.

The IRS Will Fool You if You Don't Watch Out

When I first discovered that filing a tax return was voluntary, I called the IRS and asked, "Is filing a tax return based on voluntary compliance?" "It is," I was told. "In that case," I said, "I don't want to volunteer." "You *have* to volunteer," I was informed; "If I have to volunteer," I replied, "wouldn't that make compliance compulsory and not voluntary?" "No," the agent answered, "Voluntary compliance is similar to our motor vehicle laws; you voluntarily stop at a red light—but if you don't, you get a ticket." I objected to this stating that since I could be ticketed, stopping at a red light was compulsory. "No," the agent insisted, "You stop voluntarily." (I presume that his reasoning was based on the fact that nobody was physically in the car with me, forcing me to stop.) You can see that the agent was trying his hardest to confuse me—although perhaps he himself was confused—concerning the real meaning of "voluntary compliance." He was actually trying to convince me that "voluntary compliance" was compulsory!

More recently, I called the IRS and posed as an employer who was having problems with his employees over their W-4 Forms. I explained to the agent that I had heard that I was required to send the forms to the IRS. But my employees, I continued, had said that this was incorrect and objected to my sending them in. I then asked the IRS agent to send me the law that would prove to my employees that I would be penalized if I did not send the IRS their W-4 Forms.

During that telephone interview, the IRS agent kept assuring me that I was, indeed, required to send in the forms and that he would send me a copy of the law that said so. However, what I finally received in the mail was a copy of the IRS's *Notice* 605(5-81), which tells employers that they "must send to the Internal Revenue Service copies of any forms W-4," etc., and Section 6672 of the Internal Revenue Code, entitled "Failure to Collect and Pay Over Tax or Attempt to Evade or Defeat Tax." IRS *Notice* 605(5-81) is, of course, not the law, while the section of the law they sent to me deals with employers who don't account to the government for taxes they withhold, and where employers make no attempt to secure validly completed W-4 Forms from their employees. Neither document, therefore, applied to the instant situation.

When I called the IRS back and asked the agent where in the law he sent me did it say I was required to send employee W-4's to the IRS, the agent reluctantly admitted that the section did not specifically cover that situation. He did, nevertheless, try his hardest to convince me that that law applied. Fortunately, I knew the law, so the IRS agent couldn't fool me. But, since most individuals don't know the law, they will be fooled time and time again.

The Media Plays an Important Role in the IRS's Brainwashing of the Public

Paul Strassels, who was employed for five years by the IRS as a tax law specialist, specifically comments in his book that the press is easily misled by IRS Public Affairs Officers. He writes that reporters don't usually "even know enough to ask the right questions," and that what they get is "tax law as the IRS sees it." He further observes, that "manipulating the press is easy" for the IRS.[2] I, of course, have experienced this firsthand as I traveled around the country in the last five years conducting my Untax Seminars. During these travels, I was often interviewed by the press, who then usually checked my story with the IRS's Public Affairs Officer. He nearly always convinced reporters that I was wrong (or at least confused them), despite the substantial documentation that I had always made available to them. Apparently, an IRS Public Affairs Officer is too formidable a figure to be overcome with truth alone!

Of course, around tax season, the media becomes extremely important to the IRS. Newspapers break out with rashes of stories (sent out as IRS press releases) about people going to jail or to trial for violations of income tax laws. Thus, the public's fear of the IRS and its beliefs that income tax returns are required is heightened and sustained around tax time. Also at that time, the public is constantly reminded by radio, television and the newspapers about the "April 15 tax deadline." All of this is part of a conscientiously directed government propaganda campaign designed to lead the public to believe that they are required to have their returns filed by April 15, or risk penalties.[3] The existence of this massive propaganda effort goes a long way toward explaining how the American public has been so effectively lead astray on this subject.

2. Strassels, Paul, *All You Need to Know About the IRS*. (New York: Random House, 1979), pp. 6–7.

3. As stated previously, penalties can only apply if you file late, not if you do not file at all.

Early Brainwashing—The IRS's School Program

The government's brainwashing of the American public starts at an early age. The IRS has an extensive program whereby it furnishes specially prepared materials to the public schools so that teachers can start instilling in the nation's young the fiction that they are required to file income tax returns. The program's basic publication, a 39-page illustrated tabloid that resembles a Sunday newspaper supplement, is entitled "Understanding Taxes." In the 1979 edition's "Forward to Students," Jerome Kurtz, then Commissioner of the IRS, writes:

> Our tax system relies on the cooperation of all taxpayers. It is important that each of you learn your rights and obligations. The Understanding Taxes Program reviews the historical development of our system of taxation and the vital role taxes play in our society. You will also learn the basics of tax law and have practice completing Federal income tax returns.
>
> We hope this booklet will help you better understand and appreciate the importance of our tax system.

Such government drivel explains the distorted views of government that are held by so many of the nation's young. First of all, taxes don't play a "vital role" in a society. They play a depressing and interfering role. It was precisely because taxes were relatively minor in America (until the beginning of World War II) that America enjoyed rapid economic growth, quickly achieving a position as the world's economic leader. Thus, the booklet gives students an unrealistic picture of the relationship between taxes and economic strength and vitality.

Note that Commissioner Kurtz tells the students, "it is important that each of you learn your rights and obligations" (presumably they will learn these from the booklet). Well, does the booklet explain those "rights" to the students? Does the booklet explain that individuals have a Fifth Amendment right not to submit a tax return and a Fourth and Fifth Amendment right not to be audited? No. Does the booklet explain it is the government's's legal obligation to assess each individual's income taxes? Does it tell them that if citizens wish to be helpful they can voluntarily assess their own taxes, but they might lay themselves open to IRS audits or to possible charges of tax evasion, if they do? Does the booklet explain any of this? Of course not, since the last thing this piece of government propaganda wants to do is teach students their "rights" concerning federal income taxes. The pamphlet's purpose is not to advise the students of their "rights and obligations," but to mislead them concerning those "rights and obligations." There are numerous examples of this throughout the booklet, but let me offer the one that appears on page 12 under the chummy caption of "Betty's Wages and Tax Withholding":

> Because she earned at least $2,950 during the year, Betty *must* file a federal income tax return. She will use form 1040A because all of her income came from wages reported on Form W-2.

The word "must" was, of course, used to convince students that tax returns are "required." Those writing the pamphlet knew that returns are not required, so they could not legally state that returns are "required." However, by italicizing the word "must," they were able to make the strongest possible suggestion that returns are "required," without actually saying so.

If I could cross-examine former Commissioner Kurtz under oath on this paragraph, I'm sure the examination would be similar to the following imaginary interview:

Schiff: Are individuals required to file income tax returns?

Kurtz: No, they are not.

Schiff: Now, Commissioner, I ask you to read this excerpt from the IRS publication *Understanding Taxes*, under the caption "Betty's Wages and Tax Withholding." (Commissioner reads paragraph.) Tell me, Commissioner, does that paragraph mean that Betty is *required* to file a tax return?

Kurtz: No, it does not.

Schiff: What does it mean?

Kurtz: It means that Betty can file a return if she wants to.

Schiff: Is that what you believe that students will assume that "*must*" means?

Kurtz: I can't help what they might assume. The statement itself is not in conflict with the law, since it doesn't say that Betty is "required" to file a return.

Schiff: Why, then, was the word "must" shown in italics?

Kurtz: I plead the Fifth on that question.

Another problem with the booklet is that the statement that all of Betty's "income came from wages," will not be explained correctly. Like practically all other Americans, the students will erroneously believe that "income" and "wages" are synonymous for tax purposes. So, while U.S. tax law does not provide for a direct tax on wages, students will easily be misled by this pamphlet to believe that it does.

Suprisingly, though, a wee bit of truth does manage to find its way into the booklet, somewhat like a pearl tucked away in the folds of an oyster—except that this pearl will hardly be noticed by either the students or their teachers, even if they look right at it. For example, on page 5 there is a two-paragraph statement under the heading "Voluntary Compliance and Self-assessment," which reads:

> Two aspects of the federal income tax system—*voluntary compliance with the law and self-assessment of tax*—make it important for you to understand your rights and responsibilities as a taxpayer. "Voluntary compliance" places on the taxpayer the responsibility for filing an income tax return. *You must decide whether the law requires you to file a return. If it does you must* file your return by the date it is due. You also may have to determine the amount of your tax liability. You either must pay any tax due or request a refund if you have overpaid your tax.
>
> This publication outlines your responsibilities under the nation's income tax laws. It also explains by using examples, how to fill out income tax returns and other forms you will be required to file under various conditions. (emphasis added)

Here the students are technically told that our tax system somehow involves "voluntary compliance" and "self-assessment," but are these concepts explained? Not at all. I doubt that even a minute of classroom time has been spent discussing these concepts, if they have been mentioned at all. The two terms were obviously included in the pamphlet so the IRS could just about get within the law. The IRS could claim that the students were technically advised that filing returns is voluntary and that people are expected to assess themselves, but if the meaning of these two terms didn't penetrate, that was the students' problem.

The meaning, of course, couldn't have penetrated because these two concepts, I suggest, were deliberately buried in language that was designed to mislead the students. "Voluntary compliance," the students are told, "places the responsiblity for filing an income tax return on the taxpayer." How many teachers, I wonder, flew to their dictionaries at this point to check out the meaning of the word "voluntary"? A good explanation might say something like, "Voluntary compliance means that no citizen has a legal obligation to file a return, but it would be helpful, and apprecieated by the federal government, if each citizen did assess his own taxes." Such an explanation might further mention that it is the government's responsibility to determine each citizen's tax, whether a citizen files a return or not. That, of course, would be a statement of the true nature of federal income taxes, but nowhere in the booklet are the students given the benefit of such explanations. However, another most revealing statement is contained in the same paragraph.

> You must decide whether the law requires you to file a tax return. If it does, you must file your return by the date that it is due.

I suggest that you consider that statement very carefully, since it modestly reveals a significant truth concerning American income taxes, which was undoubtedly lost on the students. It states that individuals *must decide for themselves* whether the law requires them to file tax returns. So, if a citizen decides for himself that the law does not require him to file a return—and then doesn't file one—that is within the law! That little statement, believe it or not, provides the clue to the whole income tax riddle. Citizens are informed here that they must decide *for themselves* whether or not they are required to file. The reason is obvious; since the law never states that citizens are required to file, they must decide to do so on their own!

Of course, nowhere in the student booklet are Sections 6201, 6203, or 6303 either cited or discussed. Also, all of this tax information comes to the students within the classroom setting, which gives the impression that they are learning "truth," when, in reality, they are getting a lethal dose of government propaganda that the government hopes will keep them confused for the rest of their taxpaying lives. The real purpose, therefore, of this student booklet and all other IRS publications is to convince taxpayers to decide for themselves that they are *required* to file tax returns, since the law imposes no such obligation.

The Billion Dollar Tax Industry

Besides the obvious interest that the government has in a system of taxation that squeezes the maximum revenue out of its citizens, the system of "self-assessment" has created a powerful vested interest within the private sector—the multi-billion dollar tax industry. After all, where would H & R Block and all the tax lawyers be, if not for federal income taxes? The federal government has the perfect ally to help it keep the public in the dark—the very people the public goes to for tax advice! Is it any wonder that the public has been so thoroughly snowed?

This is not to say that there are not accountants and lawyers who have been taken in themselves. Suppose, though, that you were worried about your current year's taxes and went for tax advice to a lawyer or a CPA who really knew the truth. Would he tell you, "Look Fred, don't worry; just sit back, relax and wait for the government to bill you—and they might not get around to that for years"? How much, after all, could he charge for advice like that?

The simplest, easiest and most remunerative position for accountants and lawyers to take on income taxes is to go along with the IRS. In all fairness to accountants, however, you must realize that, since they are not lawyers, they cannot be presumed to know the law (and it is my experience that they don't).

The real function of accountants is to help business get a better grip on costs and a tighter control on internal procedures so that a business can operate more economically. Unfortunately, since accountants now spend so much time on taxes, they have little time left to focus on their primary responsibilities. This has undoubtedly been a contributing factor in America's losing much of its competitive economic edge, resulting in a significant loss of domestic and foreign markets.

Accountants prepare taxes strictly according to IRS interpretations of the law and rely heavily on Treasury Department "regulations." However, regulations are not law. While practically every accountant in the country knows that the income tax is based on "voluntary compliance" and "self-assessment," I am sure that few understand precisely what these terms mean. Some do, however, as illustrated by the following interview that was conducted with a CPA who has over fifty years of experience (the accountant's name is not mentioned for obvious reasons):

Q: Did you know that filing a tax return was voluntary?
A: Yes, of course.

Q: Did you ever tell your clients that it was voluntary?

A: No, my job is to file their returns. That's what they pay me for.

Q: I understand, but isn't it your job to tell them that they don't even have to file a return?

A: It may be, but I couldn't make a living if I told them it was voluntary.

Q: Have any of your clients ever asked you if they were required to file?

A: No.

Q: You mean that in fifty years nobody ever asked you if they legally had to file.

A: That's correct. If they knew they didn't have to file, they would never have come to me in the first place.

Q: Do you know anyone who does not file returns?

A: Yes, I have one friend who hasn't filed in eight years.

Q: Has anything happened to him?

A: No, he has yet to receive even a letter from the IRS.

Q: Did you know that being audited was voluntary?

A: Yes.

Q: Did you ever tell your clients that?

A: No.

Q: So you are pretty well aware that the income tax system is really voluntary.

A: Oh, sure. I've known that for a while

Q: I take it that your position is that you would like to continue earning a living by not letting your clients know how voluntary the whole income tax system is?

A: That's right. I'm just looking out for myself.

Tax Lawyers

Tax lawyers, unlike accountants, generally have no other function than to do tax planning and tax preparation and, like other lawyers, the more complicated the laws, the better it is for their business. Unfortunately, for the public, those laws are passed by legislatures dominated by lawyers.

Lawyers, again, unlike accountants, are presumed to know the law and have, I suggest, a professional obligation to explain the laws more fully to their clients than an accountant might. So, if your tax return was prepared by a tax lawyer, did he advise you that all of the information you were submitting to the government could be used against you by numerous agencies and departments of the government? Did he ask you if you wished to waive your Fifth Amendment right concerning all the information that you were giving the government? Did he tell you that filing an income tax return was voluntary and that you had no legal obligation to give any financial information to the government? Did he advise you that, according to the law, the government was *required* to figure out your taxes without any help from you? If he allowed you to pay taxes, did he advise you, before you sent in your return, that you have no legal obligation to send the government any money until they send you a tax bill?

If, after your tax lawyer had correctly advised you concerning all of these matters, you still wanted to send in a tax return, assess yourself, *and* send the government money that was not legally due—okay. But I maintain that tax lawyers have a professional responsibility to advise clients concerning the legal implications of "voluntary compliance" and "self-assessment," so that their clients can, at least, make an intelligent decision, based on a proper understanding of the law.

If tax lawyers have *not* been explaining things properly to their clients, it is probably because they have not been taught any differently by the nation's law schools. If the blame for the public's fleecing by income taxes can be laid anywhere, it must, I feel, be dropped squarely on the doorstep of the nation's law schools, since they should have blown the whistle on the income tax hoax long ago. I believe that there is probably not a law school in the country that teaches its students the proper significance of "voluntary compliance" and "self-assessment," or whose graduates understand the meaning of "income" as defined by the Supreme Court, or the significance of the Sixteenth Amendment.[4]

Many elements, therefore, were required in order for the federal government to succeed in perpetuating this multi-billion dollar tax hoax.

1. The cooperation of a rich and powerful professional class, operating within the private sector, but having (along with the government) a substantial financial interest in the swindle.
2. Law schools that would remain silent.
3. The help of a cooperative press that could be trusted to spread all of the IRS's propaganda without asking too many intelligent questions. And of course,
4. A federal judiciary, willing to subvert both our laws and our courts.

---

4. The Sixteenth Amendment did not "amend" the Constitution at all, nor did it enlarge the government's taxing power. It merely established the income tax as an excise.

8

Federal Judges— The Real Culprits

I have always thought, from my earliest youth 'til now, that the greatest scourge an angry Heaven ever inflicted upon an ungrateful and a sinning people was an ignorant, a corrupt, or a dependent judiciary.

Chief Justice John Marshall

The federal government could not have succeeded in pulling off its income tax caper had it not had the cooperation of a federal judiciary willing to subvert our laws in order to help promote the belief that filing tax returns was required. Over the years, innocent Americans have been illegally prosecuted and jailed on the pretense that they had violated Section 7203 (see Fig. 8–1) of the Internal Revenue Code, which federal judges and government prosecutors alleged made it a crime not to file tax returns.

You already know that the law doesn't require anybody to file tax returns (except perhaps the Secretary of the Treasury) so you should also know that all such trials must be illegal. The only questions that need answering are how can such prosecutions take place, and how can innocent people be convicted?

Federal Government Designs A "Legal" Trap

Before you can comprehend how Americans can be prosecuted in our courts for acts that are not crimes you have to understand the principle of "jurisdiction" as it applies to our courts. "Jurisdiction" is the authority of a judge to hear a case. If a judge acquires jurisdiction over a defendant, he has a good deal of power over him—even the power to prosecute and jail him illegally.

For example, if some judge were to order you to appear in his courtroom you would not have to obey him, since his relationship and power over you is no different, even though he is a judge, from your relationship with any other human being. But, should that judge acquire legal jurisdiction over you, he could have you jailed for contempt if you disobeyed such an order. How does a judge, a mere human being, suddenly acquire such power over other human beings? Actually, they agree to give him that power by not effectively challenging his "jurisdiction" when they first appear before him. Once you allow a judge to *take* jurisdiction over you, he can pretty much deal with you as he pleases.

One way of understanding this relationship is to imagine yourself in an army recruiting office. As a civilian, a recruiting officer has absolutely no power over you, and you can listen to him or not, as you choose. But suppose he convinces you to enlist in the army and you are *voluntarily* inducted. Then numerous people—including the recruiting officer—will suddenly have power over you, since by going through the induction ceremony, you submit yourself to their jurisdiction. A comparable "induction ceremony" which takes place in American courtrooms is called an arraignment. That is when an accused person is brought before a judge and asked to enter a plea to a charge. By entering a plea of guilty, not guilty, or nolo contendere, the accused signifies his willingness to accept the jurisdiction of the court, and the defendant confers on the judge enormous power over himself.

To return to our army analogy, an enlisted man returning to his base a day or two late from furlough, might have to appear before his commmanding officer at a summary court-martial to answer for being AWOL. His commanding officer, in this case, would have discretionary powers within which to deal with this infraction of army regulations. Obviously, in this instance the commanding officer would not sentence the man to six months in the stockade or bust him several ranks, but there are still very broad limits within which he could punish this offense: he could be fair or unfair; he could be lenient or harsh. If he chose to exercise his power harshly and unjustly, but within the broad limits of his power, who could stop him? No one, since he has the jurisdiction within which to exercise broad discretionary powers.

However, if the individual had not enlisted, he would not have conferred this power over himself to another human being. Similarly, once you allow a judge to take jurisdiction over you, he can exercise the same broad discretionary power over you as your commanding officer; he can use his powers justly or unjustly. If he chooses to exercise his powers unjustly (and all the other judges are agreed) who can stop him? [1]

Since federal judges have collectively conspired[2] to

1. We can only stop them by compelling them to testify, under oath, before a citizen controlled grand jury (page 165).
2. Through the operation of "stare decisis" and judicial self-interest. *Stare decisis* is the principle whereby one court will follow the decision of another court even though that decision is obviously contrary to statute and even the United States Constitution.

conduct illegal trials, the way to beat them is to refuse to give them jurisdiction. I didn't know this in April of 1978, when I unwittingly turned myself over to the jurisdiction of a federal court in Bridgeport, Connecticut. At that time I knew nothing about jurisdiction, and I still had faith in the integrity of American courts. It took me three years to understand "jurisdiction" and one trial to discover that my faith in the integrity of our courts had been misplaced.

How A Federal Court Gets Jurisdiction

In order for a federal court to acquire legitimate criminal jurisdiction over you and thus conduct a lawful trial, three elements must be present.

The United States Congress . . .

(1) must first make an act a crime
(2) fix punishment to it, and
(3) declare the court that will have jurisdiction of the offense.[3]

However, there is another way for the court to gain jurisdiction; the accused can inadvertently give the court jurisdiction *even though none of the above elements are present*. In other words, the accused can, out of sheer ignorance, actually submit to the jurisdiction of a federal court, although the court should legally have no jurisdiction. This is the mistake that I—along with others who have been prosecuted for the "crime" of willful failure to file a tax return—made.

As you will discover, the federal government never had legal jurisdiction to prosecute anybody for this

3. *United States* v. *Hudson*

"crime"; therefore, it constructed a legal trap into which innocent Americans, ignorant concerning the concept of "jurisdiction," would fall.

The three elements to this trap were:

1) A fake law was put on the books.

2) Since no crime was actually committed, victims had to be tricked into *voluntarily* appearing at their own arraignments.

3) The victims had to be further tricked into pleading "guilty" or "not guilty" to something which was not a crime so that the court could get jurisdiction when it legally should have had none.

A Fake Law—The First Component of the Government's Trap

As stated earlier, before a federal court can have jurisdiction, Congress must first "make an act a crime." Look at Section 7203 again. Does that section make *any act* a crime? It might seem so to most people, but that is only because the section contains a very clever legal illusion.

Notice that the section states that "any person *required* under this title. . . .," etc. The section, therefore, does not make not filing a tax return—or any of the other activities referred to—a crime. It states it is only a crime *if you are required* to do those things! However, since Section 7203 does not say exactly who is required, no one is brought within the language of the statute, and nobody can be guilty of violating that "law." In addition, we know that the Internal Revenue Code itself "requires" no private citizen to file a tax return—so again, Section 7203 cannot apply to any private citizen! To state this in a more technical way, Section 7203 "does not allege an offense." It makes nothing a crime! In other words, Section 7203 is a legal "optical illusion," a legal fiction!

To illustrate this in a more concrete fashion, let us compare Section 7203 (Fig.8–1) to the following Section 471 of the United States Criminal Code:

Obligations or securities of the United States
Whoever, with intent to defraud, falsely makes, forges, counterfeits, or alters any obligation or other security of the United States, shall be fined not more than $5,000 or imprisoned not more than fifteen years, or both.

Obviously, if anybody does any of the things listed in Section 471, they have broken the law. But suppose that Section 471 of the U.S. Criminal Code were worded similarly to Section 7203 of the Internal Revenue Code; it would then read:

Any person *required* under this title not to defraud, falsely make, counterfeit, or alter any obligation or other security of the United States, who with intent to defraud, falsely makes,

---

§ 7203. Willful failure to file return, supply information, or pay tax.

Any person required under this title to pay any estimated tax or tax, or required by this title or by regulations made under authority thereof to make a return (other than a return required under authority of section 6015), keep any records, or supply any information, who willfully fails to pay such estimated tax or tax, make such return, keep such records, or supply such information, at the time or times required by law or regulations, shall, in addition to other penalties provided by law, be guilty of a misdemeanor and, upon conviction thereof, shall be fined not more than $10,000, or imprisoned not more than 1 year, or both, together with the costs of prosecution.

Figure 8–1   A Legal Optical Illusion
Internal Revenue Code Section 7203

forges, counterfeits, or alters any obligations or other security
of the United States, shall be fined not more than $5,000 or
imprisoned not more than fifteen years or both.

To whom would Section 471 now apply? Who would
be "required" not to do all those things that are listed in
that section? If Section 471 were worded like Section
7203, could anyone be in violation of that specific statute?
Of course not. This is why *legitimate* criminal statutes
are never worded like Section 7203. Nobody could be
prosecuted under them—because there is a lack of jurisdiction over the subject matter. Thus, no court has ever
had statutory jurisdiction to prosecute anybody for any
"crime" under Section 7203. To lay people, of course,
Section 7203 appears to be a "law." So when lay people,
such as I, were charged with violating this "law," we
thought that we had to appear in court and present a plea
as to why we did or did not break this "law." What we
didn't realize is that in making pleas, we were accepting
this section *as law* and voluntarily conferring jurisdiction on a court to try us for breaking a law that in reality
didn't exist!

Tricking Victims into Court—
The Second Component of the Government's Trap

Often persons charged with a crime are arrested and
brought to their arraignment directly from a prison cell
so they have no choice but to appear. Others, after being
arrested, are released on bond pending arraignment. If
they don't appear, they forfeit their bond, and can also be
held for contempt. In the above examples, the individuals have no choice but to appear at their arraignment.
But I was not forced to appear at my arraignment since I
was not arrested, but on the advice of counsel,I went to

the arraignment voluntarily! I literally walked myself into the trap.

I first learned that the government was planning to do something to me on April 17, 1978, while in Tulsa, Oklahoma, preparing to put on two of my Untax Seminars. I had made a routine phone call to my office and was excitedly informed by my secretary that the media had been calling to get my reaction to what apparently was the government's move to prosecute me for my alleged failure to file tax returns.[4] The story had already been reported on local radio and television, but nothing had been told to me. My secretary couldn't give me any specifics since she only knew what she had been told by reporters, but she did tell me that the story had apparently come from the office of the United States Attorney, Richard Blumenthal in Bridgeport, Connecticut. I promptly decided to call Blumenthal to find out what the heck was going on. When I finally got through to him, he would not tell me a thing except, "Talk to your lawyer." I explained to Blumenthal, that (1) I didn't have a lawyer at that moment; (2) I had certain speaking commitments; and (3) I would appreciate his telling me what was going on—so that I could plan accordingly. He still wouldn't tell me anything.

In any event, I was on my way to the *Tulsa World* for a newspaper interview, and when I got there I explained to the reporter what little I had just learned. The reporter himself called Blumenthal and spoke to him for approximately 15 minutes. I subsequently learned from that reporter that the government was planning to prosecute me for allegedly failing to file tax returns for the years 1974 and 1975, and that, while I had not been formally

4. I had actually filed tax returns for those years (see 150).

indicted for these offenses, Blumenthal had filed an Information[5] against me. At that time, I hadn't the foggiest notion what an Information was or what my legal status was.

I was scheduled to hold Untax Seminars on the following two nights and was also scheduled to deliver a lecture a few days later at Baylor University in Waco, Texas. I now had visions of U. S. Marshals appearing at any moment and dragging me away in chains, so I did not know if I would be able to put on my scheduled seminars and/or proceed to Texas for that lecture at Baylor. That evening I consulted with a Tulsa attorney, who suggested that I probably would be able to put on my seminars and also proceed to Waco. A good deal of my confusion was resolved a few days later when my office notified me that they had received a summons to appear at the Federal Court in Bridgeport, Connecticut, on April 28th, 1978. Apparently I was a free man until then. The confusion had been caused, of course, by the IRS's desire to rush into print (on the last day of the 1977 tax season) the fact that they were going to prosecute me. Only five days earlier, I had made my second appear-

5. An Information is a written accusation of a crime, made by a U. S. attorney, which permits the government to prosecute an individual without benefit of a grand jury indictment. An indictment was required in my case because I was charged with an "infamous crime." The Supreme Court had clearly ruled in (*Makin* v. *The United States* 117 U. S. 348) that *any* crime for which the punishment is imprisonment, is an "infamous crime." "The use of [Informations] has a long history. For example, in the reign of Henry VII," writes Justice Blackstone, in 4 BL. Comm. 310, ". . . a very oppressive use was made of them for something more than a century, so as to continually harass the subject and shamefully enrich the crown." Also, as the Court observed in *People* v. *Sponsler* 46 N.W. 450, "The oppressive use of this mode of prosecution by Information occasioned struggles to procure a declaration of its illegality." In short, prosecutions by Information have long been a means of political suppression and intimidation.

ance within a couple of weeks on Tom Snyder's "To-morrow" show discussing why I had not paid any income taxes since 1973 and why other Americans might do the same. The IRS obviously was afraid that a lot of people might take my advice. Only two days before this, on April 15th, 1978, the influential *Washington Post* had run a half-page story describing my non-taxpaying activities.

"For Irwin Schiff", the story began, "April is just another pleasant spring-time month, because, while everyone else is paying taxes, he's ignoring the IRS—and so far, getting away with it." The article went on to report at length my travels lecturing against the income tax and some of my anti-tax philosophy. Concerning my appearance on the previous week's Tom Snyder show, it stated:

> "Millions watched Schiff April 6, on Tom Snyder's "To-morrow" show, hammering away on how to avoid paying up by Monday at midnight. Snyder was impressed. The audience, staff producer Bob Carman believes, may have been one of the largest in "Tomorrow's" history. At the end of the show Snyder even joked that his staff was so impressed with Schiff that they wouldn't be filing with the IRS this year either.
>
> "But I am," Snyder insisted.
>
> The next morning, nearly 2,000 miles from NBC's Burbank studios, Chicago radio commentator Paul Harvey mentioned Schiff's appearance on the "Tomorrow" show and the staff's reputed tax rebellion on his nationally syndicated broadcast. Snyder, it turned out, was just having a little joke at his staff's expense, but the public didn't know that. "Our telephones nearly broke the next morning," recalls "Tomorrow's" Carman.

The IRS wanted to rush the story into print that I was being prosecuted for my anti-tax activity, in order to counteract all the publicity I had generated because of not having paid federal income taxes since 1973 (and apparently getting away with it). The story that the government intended to prosecute me was carried in newspapers across the country on April 17, 1978—which, as I said, was the last day of the 1977 tax season—with many newspapers incorrectly reporting that I was being prosecuted for income tax "evasion."

Obviously, the IRS hoped that this story would dissuade a number of the people who had been to my lectures and had heard me on various radio talk shows during the preceeding months from not reporting or paying income taxes for 1977. On my way to Waco, Texas, a few days later I conferred with a few tax-patriots in Dallas, and we all had a gut feeling that I should not appear at that arraignment, since I had not been indicted. It just happens that, without any of us having any formal legal training, our gut feelings were right. Unfortunately, I consulted with an attorney in Dallas, who advised me—wrongly, as it turned out—to appear at that arraignment and he flew in from Dallas to represent me.

My first mistake was in voluntarily going to the arraignment. I did not know then that there would be no criminal penalties if I did not honor the summons. If a summons is disregarded, all that can happen is that a warrant can be issued for your arrest. Thus, your appearance at the arraignment is compelled, not voluntary. But before you can be arrested, someone has to swear out a warrant for your arrest and, since Section 7203 doesn't allege a crime, anybody who would swear out such a warrant would be exposing himself to a good costly lawsuit for false arrest. This would especially be true where the criminal action was initiated by Information and not by an indictment. This is why, I suggest, those charged with violating Section 7203 are never arrested, but are tricked into voluntarily appearing at their arraignment on the basis of a summons.

The Trap is Closed—Tricking the Accused into Making a Plea

At an arraignment you appear before a judge, who demands to know how you plead to the charges leveled against you. If you enter a plea of "guilty," "not guilty," or "nolo contendere," *at that moment* you "walk through the looking glass" and turn yourself over to the jurisdiction of the court. From that point on, you cease to be a free man. The judge can order you to appear in court at any time, limit your right to travel, set high bond, and, of course, you are finger-printed and mug shots are taken. You are now under the jurisdiction of the court to the same extent that an individual who goes through an army induction ceremony is under the jurisdiction of the army. After entering a plea, the court acquires jurisdiction (gets sufficient arbitrary power) which it can then proceed to abuse by making up laws that don't exist, misleading juries, denying you due process—in short, railroading you right into jail. All of the above is what happened to me and to others when we stupidly turned jurisdiction over ourselves to federal judges who, in most cases, didn't have the slightest interest in seeing to it that we got a fair trial (but for public consumption, merely went through the motions).

To prevent courts from getting jurisdiction over you, the first step is to ignore any summons alleging violation of Section 7203. Wait to be arrested. I suggest that if anyone is foolish enough to swear out a warrant for your arrest, you will have the makings of a good civil lawsuit. In any case, you want your appearance in court to be *compelled*, since you do not want to give any indication that you cooperated in *any* manner in lending legitimacy to the legal sham that would be taking place.

Once brought before the judge, you should not *under any circumstances*, make a plea; rather, you should vigorously challenge the court's jurisdiction to even try you for the "crime" of not filing a tax return.

I'd like to make this point a little clearer. Suppose you were arrested for the "crime" of eating a banana during the last presidential debate. Let us assume that 1) you don't eat bananas and 2) you didn't even see the presidential debates. Does this mean that if you were charged with such a "crime" that you should go to your arraignment and plea "not guilty"? No, because by pleading "not guilty," you would be agreeing to the existence of such a "crime" and would also be giving jurisdiction to the court to try you for it! Thus, you could ultimately be found guilty of an imaginary crime, because a jury could be instructed by the judge that such a crime actually existed! By pleading "not guilty," I had in essence enabled the court to do just that. After all, the jury would have a perfect right to assume that if I didn't believe that not filing a return constituted a real crime, I would not have pled "not guilty"!

Challenging The Court's Jurisdiction

In the above example, instead of the individual pleading "not guilty," he should have demanded that the judge show him the law that makes eating a banana during a presidential debate a crime—while refusing to enter a plea until that was done. Since the judge could not produce any such law, it would not be necessary for the defendant to make a plea and no arraignment or trial could take place.

This is exactly what I should have done at my arraignment. I should have forcefully attacked the court's jurisdiction, instead of stupidly and meekly entering a plea of "not guilty." I should have pointed out to the court that Section 7203 didn't allege an offense. Further, I should have marched right up to the bench and deposited a copy of the Internal Revenue Code before the judge and demanded that he show me where in the Code a person, such as myself, is *required* to file a tax return.

The court, of course, would not have been able to find the section, since it doesn't exist. Therefore, I could have demanded that the judge tell me by what authority he asked me to plead to a crime that didn't exist. In addition, I could have presented the court with the Garner and Sullivan decisions (see page 18) and pointed to the specific places in those decisions where the courts have ruled that those who filed tax returns are witnesses within the meaning of the Fifth Amendment. Then I should have asked the court whether the federal government can *require* me to be a witness against myself. The judge, of course, would have had to answer no, to which I could then have responded, "Then, your Honor, how could I be *required* to file a tax return, and be subject to the conditions of Section 7203?" In addition, I could have called the court's attention to Section 6103 of the Code which provides that all information on a tax return can be turned over to the Department of Justice and used against a taxpayer in all sorts of criminal and civil procedures. Then I could have asked the judge, "Your Honor, can the government *require* me to provide all of this information to the Department of Justice so that it can use the information against me?"

No matter how biased a judge might be, he would have to answer no to this question. To this I could have responded, "Then I, obviously, cannot be a person *required* to file a tax return. And if I am not a person *required* to file a tax return, Section 7203 cannot apply to me. Therefore, this court has no jurisdiction to hear this matter."

Had I and the others charged with the "crime" of not filing tax returns under Section 7203, addressed these arguments to the court at our arraignments, instead of foolishly pleading "not guilty," I doubt if any of us would have gone to trial.

One further thing. If, in this instance, a judge attempts to avoid these issues by suggesting that he will enter a plea of "not guilty" for you, on the basis that you are refusing to make a plea on your own, you should very forcefully state, "Your Honor, I am not *refusing* to make a plea. If I were shown that this court has jurisdiction I might very well plead 'guilty' to the charge, thus avoiding for myself and the government the expense of the trial. I am not refusing to enter a plea; I am merely demanding that this court show me that it has the jurisdiction to even demand a plea of me. You have no authority or jurisdiction to plead 'not guilty' for me since, if the issue of jurisdiction were resolved, I might very well plead guilty on my own." Such a position would, I believe, block any attempt on the part of a judge to proceed with the arraignment. I would *under no circumstances* allow the proceedings to continue until the issue of jurisdiction had been resolved by either that court or a higher court.[6] Remember, if a federal judge attempts to punish you in any way before the question of jurisdiction has been resolved, he can be held personally liable. A federal judge can, with apparent immunity, make all sorts of mistakes

---

6. Don't fall into the trap of accepting the court's assurance that the issue of jurisdiction "can be brought up later." You don't even want to give the court the jurisdiction to rule on the issue. You want the issue of jurisdiction resolved then and there. Refuse to move forward until it is.

when he has jurisdiction but he can be held personally liable for his mistakes when he doesn't have jurisdiction. So a federal judge will think twice about acting unlawfully before he acquires unchallenged jurisdiction.

The Privacy Act Notice Now Bars Criminal Prosecutions

In addition to the above, all citizens now have the protection of the Privacy Act Notice. Unfortunately, I was prosecuted for failing to file returns for the years 1974 and 1975 which was before the Privacy Act Notice accompanied the returns, so I could not raise this issue at my arraignment. But those who stop filing now have the formal protection of the notice which, I believe if used properly, is a total bar to criminal prosecution under Section 7203. Should any judge attempt to charge you for the "crime" of not filing a tax return, you need only take out the Privacy Act Notice and state that you *relied* on that notice as the government's assurance to you that you did not risk criminal prosecution for not filing a tax return. The government was required *by law* to notify you of the consequences of not filing, *if any,* and since they did not notify you that you could face criminal prosecution, perhaps even be fined and jailed, they are thus barred from instituting any criminal proceeding against you. When you put all of the above together, no one should be fearful any longer of being prosecuted for the "crime" of not filing a tax return.

Apart from the legal trap constructed by the government (and the total failure on the part of lawyers to correctly advise citizens), the main reason that federal judges got away with these illegal trials was the total ignorance on the part of the public and the media concerning the perversion of justice that was taking place in those courtrooms. Because of the information revealed in this book, this condition, I believe, will no longer exist and federal judges will no longer be able to mislead juries and the public with the same ease as they have in the past. For this, and all the other reasons mentioned, I don't believe that citizens need fear the threat of illegal prosecutions as nonfilers and Fifth Amendment filers did in the past.

9

Why Not *Filing is in the Nation's Interest*

The history of liberty is the history of the limitation of governmental power, not the increase of it.

Woodrow Wilson

I hope I have convinced you of the three statements made in the introduction—that no American is required to file income tax returns, be audited, or have taxes withheld from his pay. I hope that you now understand the meaning of voluntary compliance and self-assessment. For those who want to voluntarily assess themselves and pay taxes that they don't legally owe, fine—simply continue what you have been doing. Others, I am sure, will be happy to discover that they have another, more pleasant, alternative.

Unfortunately, many may feel that if they do not assess themselves and pay income taxes on a weekly or quarterly basis, that somehow the country will fall apart. Permit me to suggest the contrary. If all Americans stopped assessing income taxes on themselves, America would be far better off. Many Americans actually believe

133

that, without personal income taxes, the federal government would be totally without funds. This is not the case.

Individual income taxes only provide the government with approximately 40% of its revenue, while 60% comes from other sources such as corporation taxes, Social Security and other forms of payroll taxes; and numerous excise taxes[1], such as those on liquor, tobacco, gasoline, tires; and duties on numerous imported items.[2]

Over the last few years the government has been spending approximately 25% of the federal budget on defense, so even *without* personal income taxes, the government would still have more than twice as much revenue as it needs to defend this country which, with a few exceptions, is its only real job. Most of the other things that the government does either shouldn't be done at all, or should be left to state and municipal governments, or left in the hands of private citizens or to the forces of free enterprise and competition—the forces that built this country.

Most Americans are simply unaware of all the federal taxes that they pay in addition to income taxes, simply because these other taxes are passed on to them in the form of higher prices for the goods and services they buy. Yet, the combination of Social Security and hidden taxes the average American pays actually exceeds the amount he pays in income taxes.

---

1. All of the government's normal revenue should come from excise taxes. These taxes are economically far less destructive, and far simpler and less costly to administer.

2. The government also derives some revenue from estate and gift taxes. The estate tax, an exceedingly destructive tax, (*See the Biggest Con: How the Government is Fleecing You,* pages 153-156) is also being levied in an unconstitutional manner and I believe that anyone having a substantial estate tax problem can make a successful court challenge against it.

The bulk of these taxes is camouflaged and silently passed on to an unsuspecting public. These hidden taxes are of two types; the public is somewhat aware of one, while it is totally oblivious to the other. Taxes of the former type are those excises that are levied on the manufacture and distribution of goods and services or through such things as tariffs on imported items. To some extent, the public is aware that these types of taxes are passed on to them; but the latter type of hidden taxes totally escapes its attention. These are the taxes that are ostensibly levied on the sellers of goods and services, but which, in reality, are also passed on to the public in terms of higher prices for the things they buy.[3] For example, Americans would be outraged if they had to pay a special tax, simply because they were sick and in need of medical attention. But Americans do pay such a tax and don't know it!

Most doctors are in the 50% tax bracket, so if a surgeon, for example, wants to receive $500 for the time and trouble involved in removing your gall bladder, he has to charge you $1,000 (to keep the example simple, we are excluding expenses). So, in order to keep $500 for himself, the physician, in the above example, becomes the government's instrument to collect taxes from people who are sick and in need of his attention.

Suppose that, instead of collecting this tax in the guise of an income tax, the government simply imposed a 100% sales tax on medical treatment. In this case, the doctor in the above example, would prepare his bill showing a medical charge of $500 and a federal excise

---

3. They might also be passed on in the form of lower wages. In any case, taxes paid by the producers of goods and services get passed on to the public, either in the form of higher prices, lower wages, or a combination of both.

tax of $500. As you can see, the relationships between the parties have not changed one bit. The doctor gets $500, the government gets $500 and the cost to the patient is still the same—$1,000. But, if the transaction were *shown* on that basis, the patient would be outraged! Why, he would argue, should the government charge him $500 because he had the misfortune of needing his gall-bladder removed? The public, of course, would never stand for such a tax, but they pay it now—and don't realize it!

If serfs during the Middle Ages turned over 25% of their productivity to their lords, what does that make current Americans, who now pay better than 40% of their productivity to their lord—government? Is America truly the land of the free and the home of the brave, or has it become, rather, the land of the indentured and the home of the meek?

Taxation is one thing, but what we now have in America is the illegal confiscation of wealth in the guise of lawful taxation.

The Constitution only authorizes the federal government to collect taxes to "provide for the common defense and the *general* welfare." It doesn't authorize the government to collect taxes for the "specific" welfare of some at the expense of others, though better than half of the federal budget is now devoted to such transfer payments—a largely unconstitutional practice. The cancerous development of transfer payments in the federal budget is a direct outgrowth of the "tax-tax, spend-spend, elect-elect" philosophy promoted by New Deal politicians.[4] Well, today the nation is reaping the tragic consequences of programs wrought by successive waves of comparable political snake oil

4. Attributed to Harry Hopkins, the "Guiding Spirit" of the New Deal.

peddlers, who heeded Hopkin's advice with a vengeance.

I suggest that those Americans who fought and died to create a land where men and women would be free to enjoy the fruits of their own labor would be appalled if they saw the incredible levels of taxation that Americans now meekly accept.

Incredibly, many Americans now think that an income tax is somehow necessary for America's economic and social health. For all practical purposes, however, the income tax really only started in 1942. So, if such a tax were ever needed, how did America make it until 1942 without this tax? True, the income tax was officially put on the books in 1913, but it wasn't until World War II, when withholding taxes were first imposed as a "Victory Tax", that the income tax became significant.

Prior to World War II less than 3% of the American public paid income taxes. The income tax under which so many American workers currently strain was, in reality, a World War II tax that the politicans refused to remove once the war was over. The tax provided them with the perfect vehicle with which to loot the paychecks of working Americans in order to increase their numbers and their power and to line their own pockets.

Prior to 1942, the American economy was universally recognized as the most efficient economy in the world for producing low-cost, well-made mass-produced consumer items. Does America still enjoy that reputation? Prior to the withholding tax, were foreign-made cars and motorcycles a common sight on American streets? Prior to the withholding tax were American stores flooded with foreign-made clothing, shoes, cameras and other consumer items? Prior to the withholding tax, were foreigners buying up American businesses, American real estate, and significant acres of American farmland? Before the withholding tax, did America suffer from an energy shortage? Before the federal withholding tax, did we have 15% mortgage rates and had the dream of home ownership vanished yet? Prior to withholding taxes, the dollar was regarded as the international standard of monetary integrity and reliability. Is that the case today?

What has happened, of course, is that a destructive and parasitic class of politicians used a war-time imposed tax to drain the economic lifeblood out of the nation's private economy—and the nation cannot afford to have this drain continue a moment longer.

If you want to be totally convinced of the destructive nature of the federal government, I urge you to read my book *The Biggest Con: How the Government is Fleecing You,* which will explain in detail how the federal government has literally robbed Americans of all of their money, why all currently circulated U.S. coins and currency are counterfeit and illegal, how the government uses inflation to loot the nation's savings, and how it created the energy crisis. The book also reveals how the government hides the true extent of the national debt (the government now reports the national debt at approximately 1 trillion, while, in reality, it is closer to 10 trillion), how the government has issued fraudulent reports over the years regarding the status and solvency of Social Security, and how the government literally legislates poverty, unemployment and crime.

In short, it is the federal government that is directly responsible for the nation's falling standard of living and its financially bankrupt condition.[5] The more taxes Americans send to Washington, the worse the situation will become.

5. See Chapter 5 of *The Biggest Con:*, "How And Why The Government Declared Bankruptcy and Concealed It."

As far as the government needing to pay for all of its so-called welfare programs is concerned, if it weren't for the government draining so much wealth out of each community through taxation and substantially lowering the private sector's ability to produce goods and services through pernicious legislation, there never would have been a need for all of those programs. In other words, it has been the cancerous growth of government since the 1942 adoption of withholding taxes that has created all of the nation's economic and social problems.

As we Americans roll back government by cutting off a portion of its funds, we will be rolling back much of the nation's economic and social problems. President Reagan is the first president in approximately 50 years who is trying to do this job, but he needs far more help than he is ever going to get from Congress—and I suggest that we pitch in and help him.

Remember that our founding fathers fought and died to establish certain constitutional rights for you. I would hate to believe that the American public would now hold such constitutional rights in such low regard that they would refuse to exercise them even against an arrogant and destructive government that long ago forgot that it was designed to be the servant of the people and not their master.

As America's most influential Chief Justice John Marshall stated long ago, "the power to tax involves the power to destroy." The question, therefore, for you to decide is whether you are going to continue to cooperate with a federal government that is obviously destroying the nation in accordance with Marshall's prophecy or whether you are going to stand up and assert your constitutional rights, and perhaps bring the Washington free spenders under control.

Today, you still have a choice.

Epilogue

An extensive analysis of my two trials, I felt, would add little to the main body of this book, except to more fully expose the partisan nature of our federal judiciary—a problem that this nation is somehow going to have to resolve. In addition, I fully realize that the government prosecuted me for the specific purpose of intimidating others, so I do not want an account of my prosecution and incarceration to discourage others and thus help the government achieve its intended purpose. I cannot stress too strongly that, had I known the material in this book at my arraignment (and had I not filed Fifth Amendment returns), my trial and subsequent incarceration could never have taken place.

I am including this section in the book to bring the record of my prosecution up-to-date and to focus more fully on what I regard as the underlying cause of all of the nation's problems—the refusal of the federal judiciary to *enforce the laws* that apply to the federal government.

A Short History Of "My Crime"

In 1974, while doing research for my book, *The Biggest Con*, I came across the case of *United States* v. *Sullivan*. Manley S. Sullivan was a South Carolina auto dealer who supplemented his auto income by selling moonshine. Since selling moonshine during prohibition was definitely against the law, Sullivan could have been prosecuted had he volunteered this information to the government. Sullivan decided that it made no sense whatsoever to file a tax return, since doing so would necessarily expose him to criminal prosecution; if he admitted to earning money from his illegal business he could be prosecuted for bootlegging, while if he failed to report his illegal income, he could be prosecuted for income tax evasion (and perhaps suffer the same fate as Al Capone). So, Sullivan did what any sensible person would do under the circumstances—he filed no return at all. The minions of the law, however, caught up with Sullivan and charged him with the crime of willfully failing to file a tax return.

Now, it is important to understand that Sullivan filed absolutely no return at all and was subsequently convicted of that "crime." He appealed his conviction to the Fourth Circuit Court of Appeals which, on May 16, 1927, reversed his conviction on the grounds that the protection against self-incrimination afforded by the Fifth Amendment furnished Sullivan with a "complete defense" to a charge of willful failure to file a tax return[1]

In one of the most judicially honest opinions that I have ever read, in reversing Sullivan's conviction the appellate court stated:

1. Requiring Sullivan to file a tax return would be "in conflict with the Fifth Amendment."
2. The language of the Fifth Amendment must "receive a liberal construction by the courts."
3. No one can be compelled "*in any proceedings* to make disclosures or to give evidence which would tend to incriminate him or subject him to *fines, penalties or forfeitures.*" (emphasis added)
4. The Fifth Amendment "applies alike to civil and criminal proceedings."
5. "There can be no question that one who files a return under oath is a witness within the meaning of the Amendment."

1. It is important to understand that there were other reasons why Sullivan was not required to file a tax return, but the *only issue* he raised was the issue of self-incrimination. So, that was the only issue that the court addressed. Sullivan did not raise the issue of not wanting to be a "witness against himself," which was the *more fundamental* issue—so that issue was not addressed by the court.

By stating that Fifth Amendment protection extends not only to information that is incriminating, but to information that might subject a taxpayer to "fines, penalties and forfeitures," that court effectively ruled that no taxpayer, criminal or non-criminal, had to file tax returns! In essence, what this honest appellate court did in 1927 was to admit judicially that no one had to file a tax return! It did this by simply doing its job of enforcing the United States Constitution. Obviously this was an unusual decision by today's standards.

Since the decision would have sounded the death knell to the income tax, the government appealed to the Supreme Court, a court that could be trusted to be more attentive to its needs. Sure enough, the Supreme Court reversed the appellate court's decision and sustained Sullivan's conviction—thereby giving the income tax a reprieve.

The Supreme Court Saves the Income Tax

In sustaining Sullivan's conviction, Oliver Wendell Holmes, who wrote the short opinion for the Court, did not contradict any of the observations contained in the appellate opinion, but merely stated that Sullivan's error was in not filing any tax return at all. Holmes said that Sullivan should have filed a tax return and claimed the Fifth on the return itself.

Specifically, Holmes wrote:

> If the form of return provided called for answers that the defendant was privileged from making he could have raised the objection in the return, but could not *on that account* refuse to make any return at all. We are not called on to decide what, *if anything*, he might have withheld. Most of the items warranted no complaint. It would be an extreme if not an

> extravagant application of the Fifth Amendment to say that
> it authorized a man to refuse to state the amount of his
> income because it had been made in crime. But if the defend-
> ant desired to test *that or any other point* he should have
> tested it in the return *so that it could be passed upon.* (empha-
> sis added)

It should again be noted that Sullivan did not raise
the issue of not wanting to be a witness against
himself—he only raised the lesser issue of self-
incrimination. Therefore, the Court treated Sullivan's
claim as if he were a subpoenaed witness, who failed to
appear, because his testimony, if given, would incriminate him.

An individual in that situation would be in error,
since he would have had to appear in order to claim the
Fifth. But this situation is not really analogous to the
filing of a tax return, since a filer is *not* a subpoenaed
witness, and he is the target of the questions being
asked. The Supreme Court, however (for the benefit of
the government), adopted the erroneous position that
the situations were similar, simply because Sullivan
had advanced the *wrong* issue. He should have claimed
that filing a return violated his Fifth Amendment right
not to be a witness against himself rather than claiming that filing violated his privilege against self-
incrimination. Had he raised the right issue, the Supreme Court could not have reversed the appellate
court's decision, and the income tax would have been
over long ago. This is clear from Holmes' opinion.

Holmes did not say that Sullivan had to file a tax
return, which is what current appellate and trial courts
proclaim that Holmes said in this decision. Note the
three words "on that account." Had Holmes meant to
say that Sullivan had to file a tax return, he would have

left those three words out. Then the sentence would have read, "If the form of return provided called for answers the defendant was privileged from making he should have raised the objection in the return, but could not refuse to make any return at all." But the Supreme Court did not say that. The Supreme Court said that he could not "on that account" refuse to file a return—on the issue of *self-incrimination.* On this particular issue, he had to file a return in order to claim the privilege! Had Sullivan raised the correct issue, that of not wanting to be a witness against himself, then, "on that account," he would not have had to file!

Nevertheless, federal courts now maintain that the Court in the Sullivan decision mandated that individuals are required to file tax returns—which the court did not say! But note that the Court did say that when filing a return taxpayers can claim the Fifth to *any* question "Most of the items" (questions), Holmes suggested, "warranted no complaint," although Holmes added that it would be "an extreme if not extravagant application of the Fifth Amendment to say that it authorizes a man to refuse to state the *amount* of his income because it had been made in crime." Still, "if the defendant desired to test *that or any other point,*" he could have done so!

The point is, that even while the Supreme Court's decision was far more favorable to the government than the appellate court's decision, Holmes maintained that (1) Americans could legally claim the Fifth to any question on a tax return, and (2) such claims to Fifth Amendment protection would have to be "passed upon" by a court. Although these two principles have never been overturned by any other Supreme Court decision, they are totally ignored by all federal courts today! So while the Supreme Court in Sullivan sought to erroneously restrict a citizen's Fifth Amendment protection with regard to a tax return, today's federal courts, by totally ignoring these two aspects of that decision, have sought to eliminate Fifth Amendment protection entirely!

When Holmes said that a Fifth Amendment claim had to be "passed upon," he meant that a hearing would have to be held before a judge, who would, at that time, pass upon the validity of the claim. At such a hearing, the person asserting his Fifth Amendment right on his tax return could claim that he did so based upon his belief that the information, if given, could either "incriminate him" or subject him to "fines, penalties or forfeitures."

Theoretically, the judge at the hearing could rule that the claim to Fifth Amendment protection was erroneously taken (although I fail to see how a judge could make such a determination) and then order the individual to supply the information or be held in contempt of court. But even in this case, the judge would have to give the taxpayer immunity in exchange for the compelled information.

Even the Supreme Court did not say in *United States* v. *Sullivan* that an individual who claimed the Fifth on a tax return *was breaking the law* or that the government could file criminal charges against him on the outrageous pretext that he had not filed any return at all! Nor did the Supreme Court say in this decision that the Fifth Amendment could only be claimed for certain specific questions on the return. Incredibly, lower courts now allege that the Supreme Court's ruling in the Sullivan case meant that the Fifth Amendment can only be taken on the question of the source of one's income and nothing more!

Before proceeding, let me digress a moment to explain how the "game of law" is really played in our courts. First of all, the public has been anesthetized to believe that it is the Supreme Court's function to "interpret" the Constitution. Well, that is nonsense. The Supreme Court's job is to *enforce* the Constitution, *not to interpret it.* Why should the Constitution need interpreting —is it written in Chinese?

Our founding fathers were very literate men who knew they were writing the law of the land, and they wrote it so that people could understand it. If the Constitution has to be *interpreted* that means that it is *vague,* so the Constitution would be "void for vagueness." Besides, the Supreme Court long ago stated that "where the words of the Constitution are clear, the Constitution means what it says."

However, like any other written document that establishes powers and rights among different parties and levels of government, conflicts can arise where the Court's guidance will be necessary. I recognize that constitutional issues may from time to time have to be resolved by a court, but many clauses in the Constitution are perfectly clear and so don't have to be "interpreted"—they only have to be enforced. However, lawyer friends of mine keep telling me, "The Constitution means what the Supreme Court says it means." [1] Even that is a fiction, since the Constitution is not enforced based upon Supreme Court interpretations, but upon appellate court interpretations of Supreme Court interpretations! This is what the American public does not understand.

Citizens who read Supreme Court decisions and act accordingly, may find out later that appellate courts

1. This is why, I guess, so few lawyers ever bother to read the Constitution. They apparently are taught that one has to be a Supreme Court justice before one can understand it.

do not follow these decisions and so they get convicted. When they later appeal to the Supreme Court, the Supreme Court declines to hear the case!

The game that is being played in our federal courts is as follows: The Supreme Court makes decisions which only bend the Constitution a little out of shape in favor of the federal government. It is these decisions, of course, that get reported in the press. If a Supreme Court decision is really bad, it could get a lot of unfavorable publicity. However, if, after the Supreme Court makes its decision, the appellate courts interpret and apply that decision in a totally off-the-wall manner, who knows about it? And if, as time passes, the Supreme Court refuses to hear appeals involving appellate courts' perversions of its earlier decisions, then upon what is our law based? The Constitution? Hardly. "Law" is not based on what the Constitution says, or even on what the Supreme Court says the Constitution says, but is based on what the appellate courts *say* the Supreme Court said the Constitution says. In many cases, any similarity between that and what the Constitution really says is purely coincidental!

Fifth Amendment Returns

Based on my understanding of the Sullivan case, I filed Fifth Amendment returns for the years 1974, 1975, and 1976. By 1977, however, I became convinced that Americans did not have to file tax returns at all, so I stopped filing altogether in 1977. This understanding on my part was totally confirmed when, in April of 1980, I discovered those "secret" Code Sections—6201, 6203, 6303, and 6020.

When U. S. Attorney Blumenthal charged me with

failure to file returns for 1974 and 1975, the charge was false. I *had* filed returns for those years but claimed the Fifth Amendment, instead of giving the IRS any tax information, in accordance with the Supreme Court holding in the Sullivan case. However, although my returns were perfectly legal, they were used by the government as a basis for my prosecution.

My prosecution was illegal on a number of grounds. For one thing, how can an American court prosecute anybody for the "crime" of simply claiming a constitutional right? As unbelievable as this may sound, the federal judiciary has actually made the claim of a constitutional right a *crime punishable by fine and imprisonment!* For example, at my first trial held in Bridgeport, Connecticut in February of 1979, Judge T. F. Gilroy Daly stated to the jury, "Now as you are aware, the defendant in this case cited the Fifth Amendment on his tax returns for the years in question."

Here, Judge Daly admits that I filed tax returns "for the years in question," so I could not, obviously, have been prosecuted for the "crime" of not filing tax returns for those years. I was prosecuted for the "crime" of claiming the Fifth on the returns that I did file! If the United States Congress ever passed a law making what I did a crime, the Supreme Court would have to strike such a law down as unconstitutional. So, what the United States Congress could not accomplish by legislation, federal judges accomplished by deceit.

The following is quoted from Judge Daly's charge to the jury:[1]

---

1. A judge's charge to the jury is the court's explanation to the jury of the applicable law prior to its retiring to deliberate on a verdict.

With respect to the first element of the offense charged, I instruct you that a person is required to make a federal income tax return for any calendar year for which he has gross income in excess of a certain amount of money . . . .

The defendant, Mr. Schiff, is a person required to file a return if his gross income for the calendar year '74 exceeds $2,050 . . . . Thus the Fifth Amendment does not give a person the right to withhold the required information on the return concerned— the disclosure of which would not incriminate or tend to incriminate him. However, even if the *source* of all or a portion of the defendant's income may have been *privileged* under the Fifth Amendment, the *amount* of that income, if you find that the defendant received income, was *not privileged* under the Fifth Amendment, and he was *required* to include on the return form the *amount* of income.

All of the above instructions given to the jury as "law" were untrue, but this is how federal judges go about fabricating law and sending people to prison because of it!

Judge Daly further charged the jury:

In determining the element of willfulness, you must also consider that a defendant who makes a *valid claim* of his Fifth Amendment right against compulsory self-incrimination or a defendant who makes a good faith, but erroneous, claim of the right cannot be convicted of willfully failing to make a return.

Even if you find that the defendant *erroneously* claimed his Fifth Amendment privilege, his conduct is not willful if you find that he acted in accordance with a good faith misunderstanding of the law . . . .

Judge Daly instructed the jury that I could not be convicted if I made a "valid claim" of my Fifth Amendment right and, if the jury found that I had "erroneously" claimed my Fifth Amendment "privilege," they could not convict me if I had acted in good faith.

At this point, Judge Daly was asking the jury to decide a question of law—a question that was for the court to decide and not the jury! How could a jury, untrained in the law, be expected to know if I had made a "valid" claim of my Fifth Amendment right on my tax return or if I had claimed that right "erroneously"? That was the very question that, in the Sullivan case, the Supreme Court specifically stated had to be decided by a court. However, no court had ever made such a determination in my case. Judge Daly had conveniently ducked his responsibility to do so and passed it on to a jury, who had not the foggiest idea (as he well knew) of what he was talking about.

These few examples of the court's violations of the law in my first trial by no means exhaust all of the misstatements of law and violations of due process committed by Judge Daly, but are merely offered as samples.

My First Conviction Reversed

The Second Circuit Court of Appeals reversed my first conviction, because it ruled that the trial court should not have admitted into evidence the tape of the Tom Snyder "Tomorrow" show. The appeals court noted that neither Tom Snyder nor the other guest on the show, James Schnake, who was introduced as a trial attorney and a former Chief of the Criminal Division of the United States Attorney's Office in northern California, were "sworn or qualified witnesses." Yet both of these "witnesses . . . emphasized that appellant Schiff could not possibly believe his own arguments, the very issue left for the jury." The court observed that "the jury saw the defendant's views mocked and discredited as incredible before he could speak for himself."

By reversing my conviction on the basis of a highly prejudicial television tape, the Court of Appeals was able to reverse my conviction without threatening the income tax system.

My Second Trial

My second trial was held in Hartford, Connecticut, in June of 1980, before the senior federal judge in the district, T. Emmet Clarie. Judge Clarie made so many errors in my second trial that it would take a book far larger than this one just to cover them all. Suffice it to say that, as appalling as the court's conduct was at my first trial, its conduct was even worse at my second trial. I am making no attempt to cover all of the illegal acts and blatant denials of due process committed by the courts that were involved in my second "trial" and "appeal." These courts included the U. S. Federal District Court in Hartford, Connecticut, the Second Circuit Court of Appeals sitting in New York City, and the Supreme Court itself. I simply could not do justice in this epilogue to all of the acts of judiciary skulduggery that were involved. I hope that one day I will be able to cover them in depth so that the judicial rape that took place can be revealed with all of its gory details. But if there is any skeptic who desires hardcore proof of the perfidious nature of our federal judiciary, I am fully equipped to supply it. My 1400-page trial transcript and all of my appeal briefs, including the government's replies, are available up to and including the government's response to my petition for a writ of certiorari to the Supreme Court, as well as the federal courts suspension of habeus corpus relief.

There were, however, a number of unusual aspects to my trial. First of all, the U. S. Attorney objected to my cross examination of IRS agents on tax law on the grounds that, since they were not lawyers, they were not qualified to answer questions on the law! So, while IRS agents and employees routinely make pronouncements on tax law to the public, especially during audits, the U. S. Attorney at my trial objected to their testimony on the grounds that they were *incompetent* to discuss those laws—and the government's objection was sustained by the court!

Another unusual aspect of my trial was reported in the June 23, 1981 issue of the *National Law Journal,* as follows:

> During his two-week trial on charges of failing to file adequate tax returns for the years 1974 and 1975, he amused and entertained the jury and a courtroom full of admirers. The spectacle included Mr. Schiff's performance as his own lawyer, alternately asking and answering his own questions.

The reason I had to "ask and answer" my own questions is that Judge Clarie refused to allow me to have the assistance of trial counsel as guaranteed by the Sixth Amendment. This alone was grounds for reversal! Describing this highly unusual procedure, the *Journal* article continued:

> The most unusual aspect of the trial was undoubtedly the sight of Mr. Schiff questioning himself on the witness stand. Judge Clarie, repeatedly saying he was not going to let

Mr. Schiff conduct a seminar on constitutional theory, said defense testimony must be elicited in the form of questions so that prosecutor Hartmere could object to those that were irrelevant.

So the defendant was left talking to himself, a process that lasted most of two days.

The defendant would say, for instance, "Mr. Schiff, could you please tell us something of your background and activities prior to 1974?"

"Yes, I can," he eagerly responded in a slightly higher-pitched voice. Then he narrated his beliefs and activities at length.

Judge Clarie ruled at my trial that an income tax return is filed voluntarily, even though I was charged with the *crime* of not filing one! His incredible ruling came about in response to the objection I raised when the government sought to introduce my 1973 tax return, (the last year that I filed a traditional return) to use against me. The government wanted to use my 1973 tax return in order to show the jury that I presumably knew how to prepare a "correct" return, so that they could charge me with "willfully" failing to do so for the following two years.

However, I objected to the introduction of my 1973 return on the grounds that, when I filed the return, I believed that it was required. However, my objection was overruled by the court with Judge Claire stating, "The court will rule that the income tax was filed voluntarily." So, here you have a U. S. judge prosecuting a citizen for not doing something that he had already ruled is done *voluntarily!*

If filing a return was not voluntary, the court could not admit my 1973 return and use it against me. After the admission by the court that filing a return was voluntary, I moved to dismiss the charges against me,

on the obvious grounds that if the court could rule that
filing a return was voluntary, it could not prosecute me
for not volunteering.

But Judge Clarie denied my motion on the grounds
that he was allowing my 1973 returns to be admitted
into evidence since, though they were filed "voluntarily," they were to be admitted as proof that income tax
returns were "required to be filed."

No, I am not making this up! It really happened in
the U.S.A.—not in the U.S.S.R.—and this classic example of "double think" will forever be recorded on
pages 99–100 of my trial transcript.

If Judge Clarie could have admitted into evidence
my 1973 return on the grounds that it was given voluntarily, then the charges against me had to be thrown
out. If the charges against me were valid, then my 1973
return could not have been admitted in my trial and
used against me. It's that simple!

On June 6, 1980, after the jury had been deliberat-
ing for a day, they sent word to the court that they had
some questions they wanted answered. One of their
questions was, "Under the law pertaining to this case,
what does 'voluntary compliance' mean?"

Here is how Judge Clarie answered the jury, and I
quote directly from the trial transcript:

>   THE COURT: The jury has two questions to ask of the
> Court. The first question is, "Under the law pertaining to this
> case, what does *voluntary compliance* mean?"
>   The second question is, "How does the Miranda case
> apply to this case?"
>   In respect to the *first question*, with respect to the first
> element of the offense charged, I instruct you that a person *is
> required* to make a Federal income tax return for any cal-
> endar year in which he or she has gross income in excess of a

certain amount of money. When a person does have gross income for a given calendar year in excess of the specified amount, the *primary responsibility* for filing a return is on the individual who had the gross income, *not on the Secretary of the Treasury,* or any Government official. In the calendar year 1974, a person was *required* to file a Federal income tax return if he or she had a gross income in excess of $2,050.00. And in 1975 a person *was required* to file a Federal income tax return if he or she had gross income in excess of $2,350.00.

Under the law, including the various sections of the Internal Revenue Code and the regulations enacted thereunder, the defendant, Mr. Schiff, *is a person required* to file a return if his gross income for the calendar year 1974 exceeded $2,050.00, and for the calendar year 1975 if his gross income exceeded $2,350.00, even though he may be entitled to deductions from that income in sufficient amounts so that no tax would be due, and the Government is *not required* to show that a tax is due and owing as an essential element of the offenses charged in the information.

The duty to file personal income tax returns rests primarily upon the individual taxpayer. In other words, there is no requirement under the law that the Government or the Internal Revenue Service initiate an administrative assessment of each individual's tax liability.

In other words, to put it another way, the *law requires* each person who comes within the category I have just read, in respect to income, to voluntarily, by their own free will, they *are directed by law to do that themselves.* The filing is something that is *required by law* of the individual taxpayer to initiate.

In that sense, and only in that sense, do we consider it voluntary, as such, the initiation of the filing of the return.

Judge Clarie's statement is, of course, a total fabrication and is quite in keeping with the rest of his twenty-four-page charge to the jury. Judge Clarie's "explanation" completely ignores, and is contrary to, the law as embodied in Code Sections 6201, 6203, 6303 and 6020. (Incidentally, his answer to the jury's "second" question was equally absurd and would have gotten him thrown out of law school had he given it there.) Notice that, in explaining "voluntary compliance," he uses such words as "required" and "directed" no less than nine times. Could a Soviet judge have performed any better? Incidentally, I would love to hear Judge Clarie's definition of "compulsory compliance" and how it differs from "voluntary compliance."

Another of Clarie's ludicrous charges to the jury was this amazing instruction:

> I further charge you that a good faith belief on the part of the defendant that the income tax is unconstitutionally applied ... is not a defense to this charge.

This instruction, along with others on the same theme, removed from the jury's consideration the one issue that they had to look for in order to declare my innocence—whether I acted in good faith or not. The court, of course, had already instructed the jury that I was a person required to file. Given that, what was the jury's job? The court had already declared that I was guilty as a matter of law. The jury's only job, therefore, would be to determine whether I had "broken the law in good faith" and, if so, to find me innocent. But here Judge Clarie instructs the jury that even a "good faith belief" is not a defense. If this is so, then why did Judge Clarie allow me to testify at length as to why the income tax was being unconstitutionally applied? If it weren't a defense, then the court allowed me to testify at length concerning irrelevant issues! But my belief that the income tax law is being unconstitutionally applied *is* a defense. Commenting on this aspect of Judge Clarie's erroneous charge to the jury, my attorney, Douglas Gil-

more, of Westport Connecticut, in his appeal brief to the
Second Circuit Court, argued as follows:

> If the trial judge could charge out of the case all the legal
> beliefs of Mr. Schiff which this Circuit recognized in the
> Court's *Schiff* (*U.S.* v. *Schiff*) there would have been little
> point of reversing his conviction originally. The Court re-
> versed because the defendant's actual belief and subjective
> intent on what he believed to be the law "had to be left to the
> jury." *Id.*, at 77. If it was reversible error for Schiff's views to
> be "mocked and discredited as incredible before he could
> speak for himself," *Id.*, at 82, it was certainly error for them to
> be charged out of the case as a matter of law. If they can't be
> mocked by Tom Snyder, can they be eliminated totally as an
> issue by the trial Court? What's more prejudicial—a talk
> show host saying Mr. Schiff's good faith beliefs are not good,
> or the trial judge saying they're not a defense?

In other words, there were actually far more
grounds for the Court of Appeals to reverse my second
conviction than there were for their reversal of my first
conviction! However, by reversing my first conviction,
the appeals court knew that it would not be affecting the
income tax system, while, by reversing my second conviction, it would have. So, lacking the requisite judicial
integrity, the three-judge panel of the Second Circuit
Court of Appeals affirmed my conviction orally on January 28, 1981. The presiding judge, Ellsworth A. Van
Graafeiland,[1] reading from notes obviously prepared
prior to my "hearing," *immediately* ordered my incar-

---

1. The other judges on the panel were J. Edward Lumbard and Amalya L.
Kearse. Inscribed on the terse, one-page notice that I subsequently received
affirming my conviction was this message: "Since this statement does not
constitute a formal opinion of this court and is not uniformly available to all
parties, it shall not be reported, cited or otherwise used in unrelated cases
before this or any other court." Apparently, this is how appellate courts
sweep their dirty work under the rug!

ceration, even though the court knew that I was far from having exhausted all of my appeal remedies.

I entered federal custody on February 20, 1981. On April 26, 1981 the Court of Appeals rejected my request for a hearing *en banc*.[1] On June 18, 1981 I filed a petition to the Supreme Court for a writ of certiorari.[2] On July 7, 1981 I was released from federal custody, but the Supreme Court did not deny my petition for certiorari until October 5, 1981—three months after I had already completed my prison term!

Of course, how could the Supreme Court have heard my case? They had consented to my incarceration prior to having exhausted all of my appeal remedies. Would a reversal now return to me the months I had spent locked up? Could the Supreme Court approach my appeal objectively after it had a hand in sending me to jail? Obviously, the Supreme Court had to deny my petition in order to hide its own guilt for allowing me to be sent to prison (on a misdemeanor) in the first place! How many Watergate defendants, do you suppose, went to jail before having exhausted all of their appeal remedies?

I had petitioned the Supreme Court on the basis of only one of the seventeen issues that we presented to the Second Circuit Court of Appeals.[3] I went up to the Supreme Court on the bread-and-butter legal issue (hav-

1. Appeals before appellate courts are heard before three-judge panels. However, the losing party may request a rehearing (termed *en banc*) before all the judges in the appeals court.

2. A petition for certiorari is a request (supported by a legal brief) to the Supreme Court to hear an appeal from an adverse lower court decision.

3. I appealed on only one issue because of financial expediency. In addition, my attorney felt that the particular issue was so significant that if the Supreme Court would not grant certiorari on this issue it wouldn't grant certiorari on any issue. My attorney was right—except the Supreme Court would not accept certiorari in my case on *any* issue.

ing nothing to do with taxes) upon which there was disagreement and conflict both between and within the various circuits and which could only be resolved by the Supreme Court. But Douglas Gilmore's briefs were so formidable in exposing the trial court's error that the Supreme Court would have been forced to reverse my conviction in order to resolve the judicial conflict my trial uncovered. So, despite my handing the Supreme Court an issue unrelated to taxes that literally cried for its attention, the Court let the issue go unresolved because resolving it would have gained my aquittal.

Federal Court Suspends Writ of Habeas Corpus

Though the Constitution provides that "the writ of habeas corpus shall not be suspended, unless in cases of rebellion or invasion," both Judge Clarie and the Second Circuit Court of Appeals "suspended" the right of habeas corpus in my case.

While in federal custody, I submitted a petition for the writ, claiming that my incarceration violated no less than four of my basic constitutional rights and that, in addition, the trial court was without jurisdiction to even hear the case. The petition was amply supported by case law, statutes, and the citing of factual errors committed by both the trial court and Court of Appeals. Judge Clarie denied my petition, however, without a hearing and without even requiring that the government respond to any of the issues of law and fact that I had raised.

Judge Clarie dismissed my petition on the nonsensical grounds that the issues I raised were either "raised at trial" or "should have been raised on appeal."[4]

In order to give his arrogant opinion the appearance of legal credibility, he cited a few legal cases which had no real bearing on the issues I had raised.

What Judge Clarie was saying was that, regardless of how unconstitutional and illegal my incarceration was, I must, nevertheless, *remain* in prison because I had either raised the issues at trial, or *could* have raised them on appeal.

Such demonic logic not only offends common sense, but is repugnant to the very purpose of the writ itself! In addition, it was contrary to the position of the Second Circuit Court which had specifically ruled in *Grimes* v. *United States* that arguments attacking "jurisdiction . . . or claiming significant denial of constitutional rights" were validly raised by habeas corpus, "even though [the petitioner] could have raised the point on appeal and there was not sufficient reason for doing so"!

I appealed Judge Clarie's arbitrary denial of my habeas corpus petition to the Second Circuit Court of Appeals and was granted a hearing on October 19, 1981 before a three-judge panel headed by Chief Justice Wilfred Feinberg, with Justices Henry J. Friendly and Lawrence W. Pierce. The panel affirmed Judge Clarie's suspension of my right to habeas corpus on November 2, 1981—again, without handing down a written opinion though an objective study of the briefs submitted and oral arguments made would convince anyone that my appeal should have been granted. The Second Circuit Court of Appeals was again playing games with the

---

4. I had raised two of the four issues at trial, but they were arbitrarily and summarily denied without argument or opinion. Another issue, the trial court's denial of my right to counsel was misstated by the Appeals Court in oral argument. The court wouldn't even address this issue in a written opinion. The fourth issue and the question of "jurisdiction" had never been raised at trial or on appeal.

law. On the one-page notice that I received informing me that my appeal had been denied was the message:

> N.B. Since this statement does not constitute a formal opinion of this court and is not uniformly available to all parties, it shall not be reported, cited or otherwise used in unrelated cases before this or any other court.

Well, this is to inform the Second Circuit Court of Appeals that *I* am *citing* and *reporting* this case. Its docket number is 81-2154, so it will now be "uniformly available to all parties." The Appeals Court is not going to sweep this one under the rug!

Let U. S. prosecutors across the land now know that the prestigious Second Circuit Court of Appeals has handed them yet another instrument of repression. Americans are now to be denied access to habeas corpus relief, even though they are imprisoned illegally and unconstitutionally, if the issues they raise on a petition for habeas corpus have been "raised at trial," or "could have been raised on appeal." This is now obviously the law in the Second Circuit. The Second Circuit Court of Appeals reversed in *Schiff* v. *United States*, Docket No. 81-2154 the opinion it had reached in *Grimes* v. *United States*, 607 Fed. 2d 6. It cannot be that *Grimes* v. *United States* will apply to everyone else in the Circuit, but *Schiff* v. *United States* will only apply to me!

It should also be obvious that, based upon my influence on the growing national tax rebellion, if I were wrong on the law, the government would want a written opinion that could be cited and used against others. But the Appeals Court didn't hand down a written opinion because *it knew* that it was wrong on the law and didn't want its violation of the law "reported" or "cited."

Given the federal judiciary's obvious commitment to *stare decisis*[1] rather than to the U. S. Constitution—though they take an oath to uphold the Constitution, not *stare decisis*—the public must take a direct hand in the operation of our federal courts in order to restore the supremacy of the Constitution.

I am convinced that only after we remove a few federal judges from the bench (or throw a few in jail) for blatantly refusing to enforce the Constitution will sufficient numbers of others take that document seriously. The public can exercise this control over the judiciary—which obviously now considers itself immune from such control—through the power of the grand jury.

The public is generally unaware of either the purpose or the power of the grand jury. This is because government prosecutors generally keep grand juries in the dark and emasculate their independent power. In many instances, grand juries are simply reduced to acting as rubber stamps for federal prosecutors. However, this should not, and need not, be the case.

The function of the grand jury is to receive complaints and accusations of criminal wrongdoing and to hear and evaluate the evidence presented. In our federal courts these complaints and the evidence to support them are gathered for the grand jury by the U. S. attorney, but there is no earthly reason why such complaints and evidence cannot be received directly by the grand jury from private citizens!

Grand juries should understand that not only is it their responsibility to indict private citizens who appear to have committed crimes, but, historically, they have a more fundamental function and obligation—that of protecting private citizens and the total com-

---

1. Case law precedent, even if obviously contrary to the Constitution.

munity from illegal and oppressive prosecutions brought by government. If grand juries had to rely on U. S. attorneys to initiate and carry forward grand jury investigations, how could grand juries protect the public if the government itself were deeply involved in illegal prosecutions?

Let us suppose, for example, that there were a conspiracy among government employees to hold the rest of the working population in bondage, producing real goods and services for them (since government employees produce nothing of value for themselves). To make their program work, they enlisted the help of *all* government employees—those employed as judges, those employed as prosecutors, and those government employees who had the guns (those employed in the law enforcement services). What could the rest of the productive population do? Simply resign itself to such bondage? How could the productive segment of the society free itself, short of taking up arms? It clearly could not expect any help from traditional court procedures.

Federal courts, remember, are run by federal judges, who not only have the government's interest, fat pensions, and *stare decisis* to protect, but who also must guard with tenacious fidelity the lucrative law practices of their cronies in the bar. Grand juries, on the other hand, are headed and run by lay people whose only interest is to uphold the law. They can eliminate both the government and the bar from their investigation and deliberation. A grand jury can subpeona anybody it wants, including federal judges and prosecutors, who can be made to testify under oath concerning their courtroom activities (although they could, of course, take the Fifth).

By now you know that all prosecutions for willful failure to file tax returns are illegal and involve obvious violations of Sections 241 and 242 of the United States Criminal Code. Therefore, the behavior of federal judges and prosecutors who participate in such "trials" should be subject to grand jury investigations. Judges should be made to explain under oath all of the representations of "law" that they have made to the jury, while the prosecutors should be made to explain under oath all representations that they have made either to a grand jury to get an indictment, or to a petit jury to get a conviction.

In a letter that I recently sent to a grand jury sitting in New Haven, Connecticut, in which I offered to provide evidence of criminal violations of law on the part of all federal judges and prosecutors involved in my two trials, I stated:

> Since those allegedly involved in these illegal acts are part and parcel of the U.S. Attorney's office, that office will obviously not be of any help in objectively and vigorously pursuing this investigation. I therefore stand ready to assist the Grand Jury in its investigation and can examine before the Grand Jury those witnesses which it may wish to call.
>
> In this respect, my help would be far more compatible with the nature and purpose of a citizen Grand Jury than would be the help of a U.S. Attorney. It can be argued that when a U.S. Attorney (a member of the executive branch) guides a Grand Jury (a part of the judicial branch), that this is a violation of the doctrine of separation of powers. My help, on the other hand, would not violate this doctrine, but would in fact be more in harmony with what is supposedly the philosophy of our Republic—that the government is the servant of the people, and not vice versa.

As of this date, (November 11, 1981) the foreman of the grand jury has not contacted me. The foreman, of course, is being derelict in his duty, but, since I've been so involved in writing this book, I have not had the time to press the issue. I will, though, and I will also file civil lawsuits against all parties involved in my illegal prosecution.

All of this, of course, will ultimately bring me back into the same courts that have proven to be so unreliable in the past, but we have to keep on trying, nevertheless.

What the country needs is a few grand jury foremen with some backbone! If you reside in a community where an American citizen has been convicted for willful failure to file an income tax return—and you know that such trials are illegal—you should get the name of the foreman of the grand jury from the clerk of the closest federal court and bring this book to his attention. Then request that he begin an investigation into such a trial for possible violations of Sections 241 and 242 of the United States Criminal Code on the part of those federal judges and prosecutors who participated.

I can promise any grand jury that would initiate such an investigation that we could help develop enough evidence to warrant indictments. Grand jury indictments against federal judges and prosecutors (even though U. S. attorneys might not vigorously pursue prosecutions), would still be of immense value to the nation in exposing the problem that exists in our federal courts—that of federal judges not enforcing the laws that apply to the federal government itself. That the courts did not enforce them in my case is obvious. What is not obvious is that federal courts are guilty of the same practice in *many* other areas, most blatantly in the area of government monetary policy.

Exposing our federal courts' failure to enforce the Constitution and the laws that apply to the federal government will go a long way towards helping to restore constitutional government in the United States.

Remember, the Constitution and Bill of Rights were written to protect the people from government, but if the people don't look to their enforcement, do you think the government will?

I will be available to help. Have Constitution—will travel!

Appendix

1979 Annual Report

Commissioner of Internal Revenue

This year I'm pleased to report that a number of organizational changes have been implemented and appear to be accomplishing the intended goals. The changes were undertaken last year to implement recommendations made in a study conducted by senior IRS career executives.

The change most directly affecting taxpayers was the modification of our administrative appeals procedure by consolidating the former two levels of appeal into a single appeal structure at the regional level. This system is now fully in effect and is resulting in the more expeditious handling of controversies at less expense to both taxpayers and the IRS. We continue to hold appeals conferences at all locations where district conferences were formerly held with the result that taxpayers have conveniently available to them a regional appeals officer with full settlement authority.

We believe the change in settlement procedures of docketed Tax Court cases is working effectively to utilize our resources better and to provide a more orderly procedure for handling the increasing volume of docketed cases.

The streamlining of our smallest districts has been accomplished smoothly. We are realizing savings at no loss of service to taxpayers.

Separating functions involving service to the public from those involving compliance has increased our emphasis on taxpayer service as well as permitted better integration of our collection activities with related compliance functions.

Notwithstanding our increased emphasis on taxpayer problems, it seems clear that some of these will continue to "slip through the cracks." If this occurs in even a very small percentage of the huge number of matters we handle the number of such cases will be large. To address this problem we instituted our problem resolution program (PRP) on an experimental basis in 1977 to provide a separate function to handle persistent taxpayer problems — those not satisfactorily resolved through normal channels. PRP is now fully operational in all of our 58 districts and 10 service centers with problem resolution officers who have the ability and know-how to cut through red tape quickly on behalf of taxpayers. About 72,000 taxpayer problems were successfully resolved through this procedure in 1978 and a number of systems changes identified by this program have been made to improve IRS efficiency and responsiveness.

A sample followup with taxpayers whose problems were handled through PRP found a high degree of satisfaction, but I will not be satisfied as long as some taxpayer complaints and problems persist. Therefore, as the year ended we were planning to set up an ombudsman-like position in my immediate office to have broad authority over PRP and to serve as an advocate for taxpayers.

Our forms and instructions are a matter of continuing concern. The challenge of presenting and explaining a complex law in an understandable way is formidable and we devote substantial effort to this problem. In addition to our normal work in this area we have formed a high-level task force to consider longer-range possibilities. We have engaged a private firm to review all the individual tax return forms, schedules and instructions and to make recommendations for redesign and rewriting. This effort should be completed in the fall of 1980 when we will start evaluating and testing any recommended alternatives.

While it is important that we constantly look for ways of simplifying the burden of reporting, frequent changes should be avoided. There is great value in taxpayers' familiarity with our forms. I'm, therefore, pleased that the 1979 forms follow the 1978 forms except for a few changes required by new legislation.

There is no doubt that better taxpayer assistance, more sensitive responsiveness to taxpayer complaints and problems and simpler tax forms and instructions are of great importance in achieving a high level of voluntary compliance with our tax laws. But our enforcement efforts also are crucial. Any significant noncompliance is a matter of deep concern to the IRS, Congress and the taxpaying public. Beyond the tax revenues lost when income is not reported is the basic question of fairness to taxpayers who voluntarily obey the laws.

Since the mid-Sixties the IRS has regularly measured compliance on filed returns through its taxpayer compliance measurement program (TCMP). As an adjunct to our audit program, TCMP is an effective tool to measure the unreported income detectible by normal audit procedures and to develop the

> **Doesn't it seem strange that the IRS uses the word "voluntary" _six_ times in the introduction to their own Annual Report, but does not use the term _once_ in your Privacy Act Notice?**

computer formulae used to identify returns for audit. It does not, however, measure the unreported income of those who fail to file returns nor certain types of income not readily detectible by normal audit procedures, such as income from illegal sources.

In 1978 I appointed a study group to prepare estimates of unreported income. The group's report, _"Estimates of Income Unreported on Individual Income Tax Returns,"_ was released in August 1979. This report, using data for the 1976 tax year, marks our first effort to measure unreported individual income.

The report estimates that individuals failed to report $75 billion to $100 billion in income from legal activities, with a resulting revenue loss of $13 billion to $17 billion. Unreported income from certain illegal sources — narcotics, illegal gambling and prostitution — was estimated to be between $25 billion and $35 billion, and cost the government approximately $6 billion to $9 billion in lost tax revenues.

To put these figures in context, in the same tax year individuals voluntarily reported nearly $1.1 trillion in income and paid a total of $142 billion in income taxes.

The report lends considerable weight to conclusions drawn from past TCMP studies that voluntary reporting is highest when incomes are subject to tax withholding. Incomes subject to information reporting show a lower compliance level but still much higher than incomes subject to neither withholding nor information reporting.

In fairness to the millions of taxpayers who voluntarily file, report all their income and pay the tax due, we must strengthen current compliance efforts and, where called for, plan innovative actions to find and tax unreported income.

A Treasury legislative proposal, currently under consideration by Congress, to withhold taxes from certain independent contractors would be a major step in dealing with one area of low compliance.

Our program to match information documents filed by payers of wages, dividends, interest and certain other payments with income tax returns has become an increasingly important tool to identify cases of underreporting of income and nonfiling of returns. The number of documents matched has been increasing substantially and with the full implementation of the combined annual wage reporting system will reach 400 million or about 80 percent of the total filed.

Our document matching activity has been separate from our examination program and has not affected the selection of returns for audit or their actual audit. However, in the next filing season, a printout of the information documents processed will be associated with returns selected for the examination program so that the information will be available to tax return classifiers and to return examiners. Since these documents will also be used during TCMP audits, the accuracy of the results of that program should also be improved.

In last year's report I noted our increasing concern about the use of abusive tax shelters — those which take positions beyond a reasonable interpretation of the law — and our increased audit effort in this area. As a result of that effort we have, at various stages of the examination and appeals process, about 200,000 tax returns involving about $4.5 billion of questionable deductions. This program requires a substantial commitment of resources but it is a commitment we will continue to make, and even increase if necessary. The great abuse we are finding in this area, if allowed to continue unchecked, could result in a serious decline in taxpayers' perception of the fairness and evenhandedness of our administration of the tax system and consequently in their voluntary compliance.

Many abusive tax shelters depend for their successful marketing on the participation of professional tax advisors. We intend to continue an exploration, begun this year, into the ethical and legal standards that should govern such participation.

Tax administration today calls for us to increase our abilities to serve the majority of taxpayers who comply with the law. A crucial aspect of this service is to enforce the law vigorously against the few who attempt to subvert it. We believe this year's report reflects that commitment.

Jerome Kurtz
Jerome Kurtz
Commissioner of Internal Revenue

Reading List

All books available through Freedom Books, P.O. Box 5303, Hamden, CT 06518. Please add the following amounts for mailing charges:

Under ϕ10 — add ϕ1.50

ϕ10-ϕ25 — add ϕ2.00

Over ϕ25 — add ϕ3.00

Prices guaranteed through September, 1982.

Books and Materials by Irwin Schiff

How Anyone Can Stop Paying Income Taxes. ϕ11, hardback. Will make a great gift for your lawyer, accountant or local IRS agent.

Why No One Can Have Any Taxable Income. **ϕ8.00 pre-publication price,** ϕ12.50 after publication. Anticipated release date June 1, 1982. The Manual will explain why wages, alimony, interest, dividends, rent, etc. are not taxable as "income" under the Internal Revenue Code. The Manual will enable you to challenge any attempt by the government to assess you and will provide you with a basis for amending returns filed in previous years. Memorandum of law included.

The Biggest Con: How the Government is Fleecing You. ϕ6, paperback. Provides irrefutable evidence of the criminal and destructive nature of the federal government. "The single most important book on the status of this nation I have ever read," said Howard Ruff, editor of *The Ruff Times.*

*ϕ Denotes Federal Reserve units, fiat currency now fraudulently circulating as U.S. dollars.

174

Kingdom of Moltz. ¢2.50, paperback. A delightful tale of our monetary system written so that even a child of ten can understand it. "I laughed so hard I cried. Schiff's book is the greatest thing since sliced bread," commented Dr. Camille Castorina, economics professor at St. John's University.

The Tax Rebels Guide to the Constitution and Declaration of Independence. ¢1.50 paperback. The guide is color coded to call attention to particular clauses which should be of special interest to those Americans interested in preserving their constitutional rights.

The Freedom Kit. ¢25. For those wanting the original work that ignited the tax rebellion, and upon which *How Anyone Can Stop Paying Income Taxes* is based. The kit contains 5 cassette tapes and a number of supporting documents. Formerly sold for ¢45 (while supply lasts).

Trial Transcript. ¢35. Irwin Schiff's 1400 page complete anotated transcript of his second trial. Has to be read in the original in order to be believed. "The greatest outrage ever conducted in an American court."

Appeal Briefs. ¢6.00. Contains basic appeal brief listing and arguing 17 areas of reversible error, plus the government's *Reply Brief*, and Schiff's answer. Reveals the naked hypocracy of a federal appeals court in cases involving the government's taxing power.

Other Books of Interest

The Internal Revenue Code. ¢13.00, paperback. For those who may want a copy of our tax laws, since you now know you cannot trust the IRS to explain the law correctly.

Miracle on Main Street, by F. Tupper Saussy. ϕ6, paperback. A gem of a book which explains why, on Constitutional grounds, Americans can legally stop paying state and local taxes.

A Need to be Free, by Frank Turano. ϕ5, paperback. Disproves the myth that children are legally required to attend school. Written by a Massachusetts policeman who withdrew his children from school in order to educate them at home. Fully documented with case law.

Legal Cases Cited

Ballou v. Kemp, 92 F2nd 556
Bivens v. Six Unknown Agents of Federal Bureau of Narcotics, 403 US 388
Boyce v. Grundy, 3 Pet. 210
Boyd v. U.S., 116 US 616
Brinkley v. Brinkley, 56 NY 192
Chadwick (D.C. Mass), Fed. CAS 2570, 1 Lowell 439
Cairo & Fulton R.R. Co. v. Hecht, 95 US 170
Connally v. General Construction Co., 269 US 330
Fields v. U.S., 27 App.D.C. 433
Flora v. U.S., 362 US 145
Fort Howard Paper Co. v. Fox River Heights Sanitary Dist., 26 NW2nd 661
Garner v. U.S., 424 US 648
George Williams College v. Village of Williams Bay, 7 NW2nd 891
Gow v. Consolidated Coppermines Corp., 165 Atl. 136
Grimes v. U.S., 607 F2nd 6
Makin v. U.S., 117 US 348
McCarthy v. Arndstein, 266 US 34
Miranda v. U.S., 384 US 436
Nicola v. U.S., 72 F2nd 780
Nudd v. Burrows, 91 US 426
Reisman v. Caplin, 375 US 440
Sullivan v. U.S., 15 F2nd 809
U.S. v. Dickerson, 413 F2nd 1111
U.S. v. Hudson, 11 US 32
U.S. v. Malinkowski, 347 F.Supp. 347
U.S. v. Powell, 375 US 48
U.S. v. Roundtree, 420 F2nd 845
U.S. v. Sullivan, 274 US 259
U.S. v. Throckmorton, 98 US 61